Wonderful ways to prepare

# CREPES &
# PANCAKES

by JO ANN SHIRLEY

**TITLES IN THIS SERIES**

Wonderful ways to prepare

# CREPES &
# PANCAKES

**PLAYMORE INC. NEW YORK USA
UNDER ARRANGEMENT WITH
WALDMAN PUBLISHING CORP.**

**AYERS & JAMES
SYDNEY AUSTRALIA**

**STAFFORD PEMBERTON PUBLISHING
KNUTSFORD UNITED KINGDOM**

FIRST PUBLISHED 1979

PUBLISHED IN THE USA
BY PLAYMORE INC.
UNDER ARRANGEMENT WITH
WALDMAN PUBLISHING CORP.

PUBLISHED IN AUSTRALIA
BY AYERS & JAMES
CROWS NEST N.S.W., AUSTRALIA

PUBLISHED IN THE UNITED KINGDOM
BY STAFFORD PEMBERTON PUBLISHING
KNUTSFORD CHESHIRE

COPYRIGHT © 1979
AYERS & JAMES PTY. LTD.
5 ALEXANDER STREET,
CROWS NEST N.S.W. AUSTRALIA

COVER PHOTOGRAPHY BY COURTESY OF MONIER
CONSUMER PRODUCTS
ISBN 0 86908 157 8

# Contents

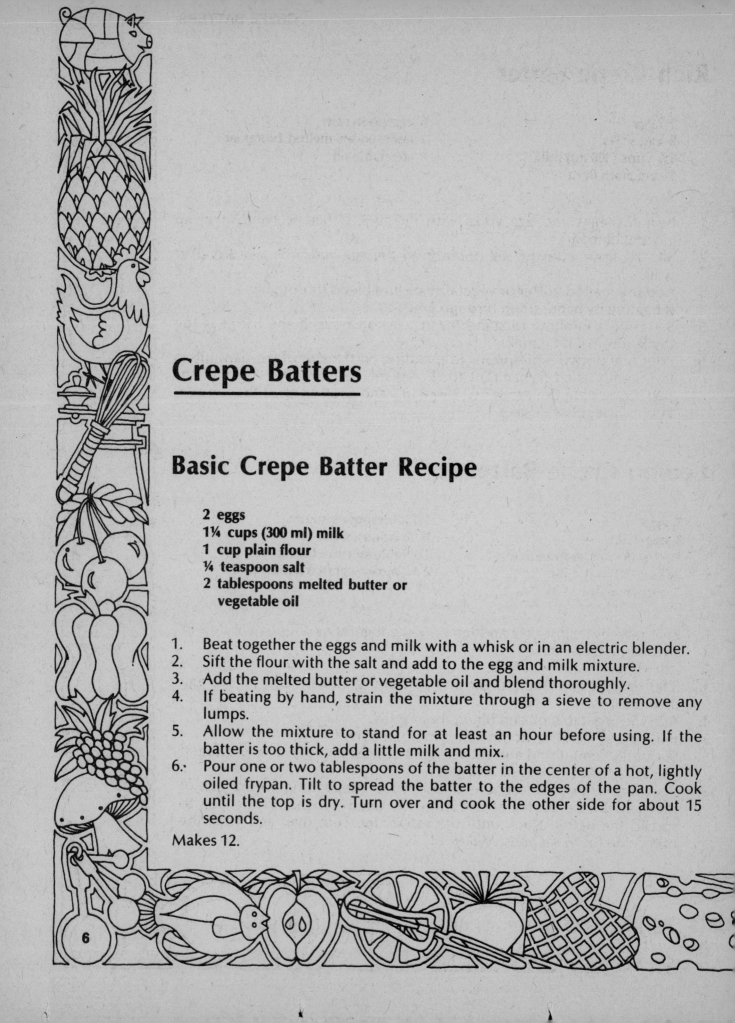

# Crepe Batters

## Basic Crepe Batter Recipe

2 eggs
1¼ cups (300 ml) milk
1 cup plain flour
¼ teaspoon salt
2 tablespoons melted butter or
vegetable oil

1. Beat together the eggs and milk with a whisk or in an electric blender.
2. Sift the flour with the salt and add to the egg and milk mixture.
3. Add the melted butter or vegetable oil and blend thoroughly.
4. If beating by hand, strain the mixture through a sieve to remove any lumps.
5. Allow the mixture to stand for at least an hour before using. If the batter is too thick, add a little milk and mix.
6. Pour one or two tablespoons of the batter in the center of a hot, lightly oiled frypan. Tilt to spread the batter to the edges of the pan. Cook until the top is dry. Turn over and cook the other side for about 15 seconds.

Makes 12.

# Rich Crepe Batter

2 eggs
2 egg yolks
1¼ cups (300 ml) milk
1 cup plain flour

¼ teaspoon salt
2 tablespoons melted butter or
  vegetable oil

1. Beat the eggs and egg yolks with the milk either by hand or in an electric blender.
2. Sift the flour with the salt and add to the egg and milk mixture. Beat well.
3. Add the melted butter or vegetable oil and blend thoroughly.
4. If beating by hand, strain through a sieve.
5. Set aside and allow to stand for at least an hour. If the batter is too thick, mix in a little milk.
6. Pour one or two tablespoons (depending on the size of the pan) into a hot, lightly oiled frypan. Tilt to spread the batter to the edges of the pan. Cook until the top is dry, then turn and cook on the other side for about 15 seconds. Makes 12.

# Lemon Crepe Batter

3 eggs
2 egg yolks
¼ cup (65 ml) lemon juice
¾ cup (185 ml) milk
1 cup plain flour

1¼ tablespoons sugar
½ teaspoon salt
1½ tablespoons vegetable oil
2 teaspoons grated lemon rind

1. Beat the eggs, egg yolks and lemon juice together either by hand or in an electric blender.
2. Add the milk and beat well.
3. Sift together the flour, sugar and salt and gradually add to the egg mixture.
4. Add the vegetable oil and blend thoroughly.
5. If mixing by hand, pour the batter through a sieve.
6. Stir in the lemon rind and set aside for at least an hour before using. If too thick, add a little milk and mix well.
7. Pour one or two tablespoons of the batter (depending on the size of the pan) in the center of a hot, lightly oiled frypan. Tip the pan to spread the batter. Cook until the top is dry. Turn over and cook the other side for 15 seconds. Makes 12.

# Orange Crepe Batter

4 eggs  
½ cup (125 ml) orange juice  
½ cup (125 ml) milk  
1½ cups plain flour  

1¼ tablespoons sugar  
½ teaspoon salt  
1¼ tablespoons vegetable oil  
1½ teaspoons grated orange rind  

1. Beat the eggs with the orange juice and milk.
2. Sift the flour with the sugar and salt and gradually add to the egg mixture.
3. Add the vegetable oil and mix well.
4. If mixing by hand, strain the batter through a sieve to remove any lumps.
5. Mix the orange rind into the batter.
6. Set aside and allow to stand for at least an hour before using. If too thick, add a little milk and mix well.
7. Pour one or two tablespoons of the batter (depending on the size of the pan) in the middle of a hot, lightly oiled frypan. Tilt the pan to spread the batter and cook until the top is dry. Turn over and cook for 15 seconds on the other side. Makes 12.

# Chocolate Crepe Batter

3 eggs  
1¼ cups (300 ml) buttermilk  
½ teaspoon vanilla essence  
1 cup plain flour  

2½ tablespoons sugar  
2½ tablespoons cocoa  
2 tablespoons melted butter or vegetable oil  

1. Beat the eggs, then add the buttermilk and vanilla essence and mix well by hand or in an electric blender.
2. Sift the flour with the sugar and cocoa and slowly add to the egg and buttermilk mixture.
3. Stir in the melted butter or vegetable oil and blend thoroughly.
4. If mixing by hand, pour the batter through a strainer to remove any lumps.
5. Set aside and allow to stand for at least an hour before using. If the batter is too thick, add a little water and mix well.
6. Pour one or two tablespoons of the batter (depending on the size of the pan) in the center of a hot, lightly oiled frypan. Tip the pan to spread the batter. Cook until the top is dry, then turn and cook on the other side for 15 seconds. Makes 12.

# Vanilla Crepe Batter

3 eggs
2 cups (500 ml) milk
2½ teaspoons vanilla essence
1⅔ cups plain flour

½ teaspoon salt
1¼ tablespoons sugar
2½ tablespoons melted butter or
   vegetable oil

1. Beat the eggs, then mix with the milk and vanilla essence either by hand or in an electric blender.
2. Sift the flour with the salt and sugar and gradually add to the egg and milk mixture.
3. Add the melted butter or vegetable oil and blend thoroughly.
4. If mixing by hand, strain the batter through a sieve.
5. Set aside and allow to stand for at least an hour before using. If too thick after standing, add a little milk and mix well.
6. Pour one to two tablespoons of the batter (depending on the size of the pan) in the middle of a hot, lightly oiled frypan. Tilt to spread the batter and cook until the top is dry. Turn and cook on the other side for 15 seconds. Makes 12.

# Spinach Crepe Batter

3 eggs
1¼ cups (300 ml) milk
¼ cup puréed spinach
1¼ cups plain flour

½ teaspoon salt
⅛ teaspoon black pepper
pinch of nutmeg
2 tablespoons vegetable oil

1. Beat the eggs, then add to the milk and either beat by hand or whirl in an electric blender.
2. Add the puréed spinach and blend well.
3. Sift the flour with the salt, pepper and nutmeg and gradually add to the spinach mixture.
4. Add the vegetable oil and beat well.
5. If mixing by hand, pour the batter through a sieve.
6. Set aside for at least one hour. Stir and if too thick, add a little milk and mix well.
7. Pour one or two tablespoons of the batter (depending on the size of the pan) in the center of a hot, lightly oiled frypan. Tilt the pan to spread the batter and cook until the top is dry. Turn and cook on the other side for about 15 seconds. Makes 12.

# Cheesey Crepe Batter

2 eggs
1½ cups (375 ml) milk
1 cup plain flour

4 tablespoons grated hard cheese
½ teaspoon salt
1¼ tablespoons vegetable oil

1. Beat the eggs and mix thoroughly with the milk by hand or in an electric blender.
2. Gradually add the flour, cheese and salt and blend thoroughly.
3. Mix in the vegetable oil.
4. Set aside and allow to stand for at least an hour before using. If the batter is too thick after standing, add a little milk and mix well.
5. Pour one or two tablespoons of the batter (depending on the size of the pan) in the center of a hot, lightly oiled frypan. Tilt the pan to allow the batter to spread. Cook until the top is dry, then turn and cook for 15 seconds on the other side.

Makes 12.

# Beer Crepe Batter

3 eggs
1 cup (250 ml) beer
1 cup plain flour

½ teaspoon salt
2½ tablespoons melted butter or
vegetable oil

1. Beat the eggs, then mix with the beer either in an electric blender or beating by hand.
2. Sift the flour with the salt and gradually mix into the egg and beer mixture.
3. Beat in the melted butter or vegetable oil.
4. If mixing by hand, pour the batter through a sieve to remove any lumps.
5. Set aside and allow to stand for at least an hour before using. If the batter is too thick, add a little water and mix well.
6. Pour one or two tablespoons of the batter (depending on the size of the pan) in the middle of a hot, lightly oiled frypan. Tilt the pan to spread the batter and cook until the top is dry. Turn and cook on the other side for 15 seconds.

Makes 10.

# Almond Crepe Batter

3 eggs
1 cup (250 ml) milk
1 teaspoon almond essence
¾ cup plain flour

¼ cup ground almonds
½ teaspoon salt
2½ tablespoons melted butter or
vegetable oil

1. Beat the eggs and mix with the milk and almond essence beating by hand or in an electric blender.
2. Sift the flour and mix with the ground almonds and salt. Gradually add to the egg and milk mixture.
3. Add the melted butter or vegetable oil and mix well.
4. Strain the batter through a sieve if you have mixed by hand to remove any lumps.
5. Set aside and allow to stand for at least an hour before using. If too thick, add a little milk and mix well.
6. Pour one or two tablespoons of the batter (depending on the size of the pan) in the center of a hot, lightly oiled frypan. Tilt the pan to batter. Cook until the top is dry, then turn and cook on the other side for about 15 seconds. Makes 10.

# Wheat Germ Crepe Batter

2 eggs
1½ cups (375 ml) milk
1 cup plain flour
⅓ cup wheat germ
½ teaspoon salt
1¼ tablespoons vegetable oil

1. Beat the eggs, then mix with the milk by hand or in an electric blender.
2. Add the sifted plain flour, the wheat germ and the salt and mix well.
3. Stir in the vegetable oil.
4. If mixing by hand, pour the batter through a strainer.
5. Set aside and allow to stand for at least an hour before using. If too thick, add a little milk and mix well.
6. Pour one to two tablespoons of the batter (depending on the size of the pan) in the center of a hot, lightly oiled frypan. Tilt the pan to spread the batter and cook until the top is dry. Turn over and cook on the other side for about 15 seconds. Makes 12.

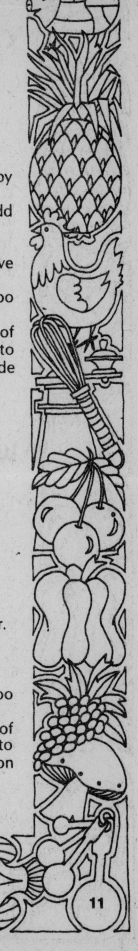

# Herb Crepe Batter

2 **eggs**
1½  **cups (375 ml) milk**
1¼  **cups plain flour**
½ **teaspoon salt**
1¼ **tablespoons minced parsley**

1¼ **tablespoons minced chives**
1¼ **tablespoons minced thyme**
1¼ **tablespoons minced tarragon**
4 **tablespoons melted butter or**
   **vegetable oil**

1.  Beat the eggs, then mix in the milk either by hand or in an electric blender.
2.  Sift the flour with the salt and add to the egg and milk mixture. Blend thoroughly.
3.  Add the parsley, chives, thyme, tarragon and melted butter or vegetable oil.
4.  Set aside and allow to stand for at least an hour before using. Stir and, if too thick, add a little milk and mix well.
5.  Pour one to two tablespoons of the batter (depending on the size of the pan) in the center of a hot, lightly oiled frypan and tilt the pan to spread the batter. Cook until the top is dry. Turn and cook on the other side for about 15 seconds.

Makes 12.

# Wholemeal Crepe Batter

2 **eggs**
2 **cups (500 ml) milk**
1¾  **cups wholemeal flour**

½ **teaspoon salt**
2½ **tablespoons melted butter or**
   **vegetable oil**

1.  Beat the eggs, then combine with the milk and beat by hand or in an electric blender.
2.  Sift together the flour and salt and add to the egg and milk mixture. Blend thoroughly.
3.  Stir in the melted butter or vegetable oil.
4.  If mixing by hand, strain through a sieve to remove any lumps.
5.  Allow to stand for at least an hour before using. If the batter is too thick, add a little milk and blend well.
6.  Pour one to two tablespoons of the batter (depending on the size of the pan) in the center of a hot, lightly oiled frypan. Tilt to allow the batter to spread and cook until the top is dry. Turn over and cook the other side for about 15 seconds.

Makes 12.

# Bran Crepe Batter

2 eggs
1¼ cups (375 ml) milk
½ cup bran
¾ cup wholemeal flour

½ teaspoon salt
2 teaspoons sugar
2 tablespoons melted butter or
    vegetable oil

1. Beat the eggs and mix with the milk by hand or in an electric blender.
2. Add the bran, flour, salt and sugar and beat well.
3. Mix in the melted butter or vegetable oil.
4. If mixing by hand, strain the batter through a sieve.
5. Set aside and allow to stand for at least an hour before using. Stir and, if too thick, thin with a little milk.
6. Pour one or two tablespoons of the batter (depending on the size of the pan) in the middle of a hot, lightly oiled frypan. Tilt the pan to spread the batter and cook until the top is dry. Turn over and cook on the other side for about 15 seconds.

Makes 12.

# Skim Milk Crepe Batter

2 eggs
1 cup (250 ml) skim milk
1¼ cups plain flour
¼ teaspoon salt
2½ tablespoons melted butter or
    vegetable oil

1. Beat together the eggs and milk by hand or in an electric blender.
2. Sift the flour with the salt and add to the egg and milk mixture. Beat well.
3. Add the melted butter or vegetable oil and blend thoroughly.
4. If beating by hand, strain the batter through a sieve to remove any lumps.
5. Set aside and allow to stand for at least an hour. If the batter is too thick, add a little milk and mix well.
6. Pour one or two tablespoons of the batter (depending on the size of the pan) in the center of a hot, lightly oiled frypan. Tilt to spread the batter to the edges of the pan. Cook until the top is dry, then turn and cook on the other side for about 15 seconds.

Makes 12.

# Sour Milk Crepe Batter

1 cup (250 ml) milk
1 tablespoon lemon juice
½ cup (125 ml) water
2 eggs

1 cup plain flour
½ teaspoon salt
2 tablespoons melted butter or
vegetable oil

1. Mix the milk with the lemon juice and set aside for 15 minutes to allow the milk to sour.
2. Combine the soured milk with the water.
3. Beat the eggs and add to the milk mixture.
4. Sift the flour with the salt and add to the egg and milk mixture. Mix until thoroughly blended by hand or in an electric blender.
5. If mixing by hand, pour the batter through a sieve to remove all the lumps.
6. Set aside to stand for at least an hour. If too thick, add a little more milk and mix well.
7. Pour one to two tablespoons of the batter (depending on the size of the pan) in the center of a hot, lightly oiled frypan and tilt to allow the batter to spread over the bottom of the pan. Cook until the crepe is dry on the top. Turn over and cook on the other side for about 15 seconds.

Makes 12.

# Cornmeal Crepe Batter

½ cup cornmeal
½ cup (125 ml) hot water
3 eggs
1 cup (250 ml) milk

½ cup plain flour
½ teaspoon salt
3 tablespoons melted butter or
vegetable oil

1. Mix the cornmeal with the hot water and set aside for ten minutes.
2. Beat the eggs and blend with the milk either by hand or in an electric blender.
3. Add the cornmeal to the egg and milk mixture.
4. Sift the flour with the salt and gradually add to the batter.
5. Stir in the melted butter or vegetable oil.
6. Set aside and allow to stand for at least an hour before using. Add a little more milk if too thick.
7. Pour one or two tablespoons of the batter (depending on the size of the pan) in the center of a hot, lightly oiled frypan. Tilt the pan to spread the batter and cook until the top is dry. Turn over and cook on the other side for 15 seconds. Makes 10.

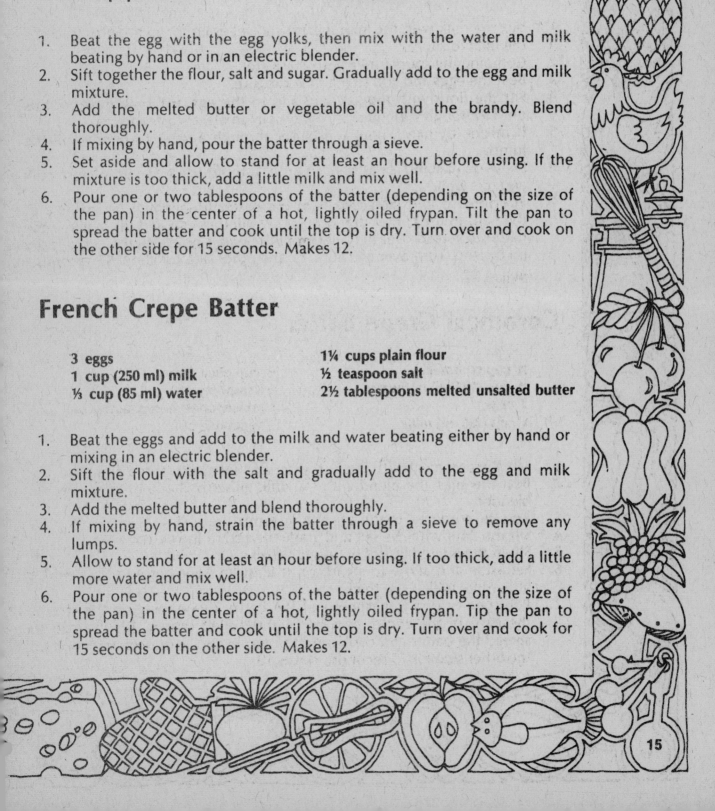

# Sweet Crepe Batter

2 eggs
2 egg yolks
½ cup (125 ml) water
¾ cup (185 ml) milk
1¼ cups plain flour

½ teaspoon salt
2 tablespoons sugar
1¼ tablespoons melted butter or vegetable oil
1 tablespoon brandy

1. Beat the egg with the egg yolks, then mix with the water and milk beating by hand or in an electric blender.
2. Sift together the flour, salt and sugar. Gradually add to the egg and milk mixture.
3. Add the melted butter or vegetable oil and the brandy. Blend thoroughly.
4. If mixing by hand, pour the batter through a sieve.
5. Set aside and allow to stand for at least an hour before using. If the mixture is too thick, add a little milk and mix well.
6. Pour one or two tablespoons of the batter (depending on the size of the pan) in the center of a hot, lightly oiled frypan. Tilt the pan to spread the batter and cook until the top is dry. Turn over and cook on the other side for 15 seconds. Makes 12.

# French Crepe Batter

3 eggs
1 cup (250 ml) milk
⅓ cup (85 ml) water

1¼ cups plain flour
½ teaspoon salt
2½ tablespoons melted unsalted butter

1. Beat the eggs and add to the milk and water beating either by hand or mixing in an electric blender.
2. Sift the flour with the salt and gradually add to the egg and milk mixture.
3. Add the melted butter and blend thoroughly.
4. If mixing by hand, strain the batter through a sieve to remove any lumps.
5. Allow to stand for at least an hour before using. If too thick, add a little more water and mix well.
6. Pour one or two tablespoons of the batter (depending on the size of the pan) in the center of a hot, lightly oiled frypan. Tip the pan to spread the batter and cook until the top is dry. Turn over and cook for 15 seconds on the other side. Makes 12.

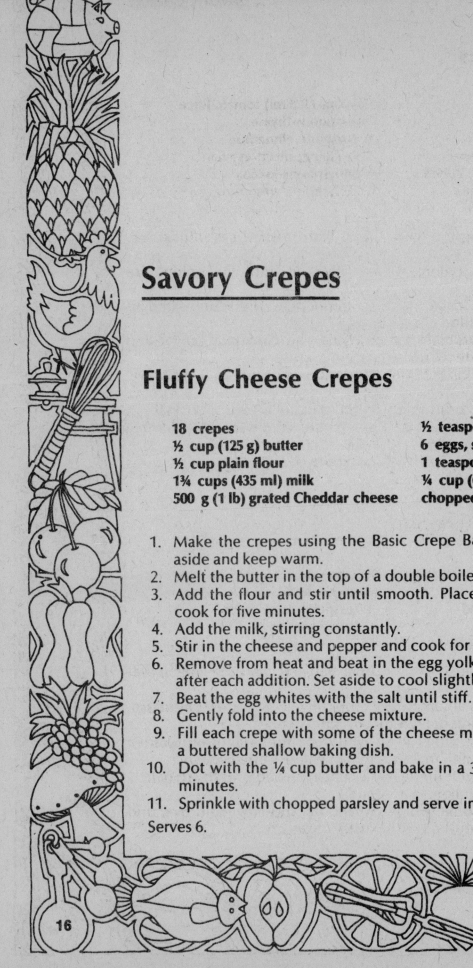

# Savory Crepes

## Fluffy Cheese Crepes

18 crepes
½ cup (125 g) butter
½ cup plain flour
1¾ cups (435 ml) milk
500 g (1 lb) grated Cheddar cheese

½ teaspoon black pepper
6 eggs, separated
1 teaspoon salt
¼ cup (65 g) butter
chopped parsley

1. Make the crepes using the Basic Crepe Batter recipe (see Index). Set aside and keep warm.
2. Melt the butter in the top of a double boiler.
3. Add the flour and stir until smooth. Place over simmering water and cook for five minutes.
4. Add the milk, stirring constantly.
5. Stir in the cheese and pepper and cook for another five minutes.
6. Remove from heat and beat in the egg yolks one at a time, beating well after each addition. Set aside to cool slightly.
7. Beat the egg whites with the salt until stiff.
8. Gently fold into the cheese mixture.
9. Fill each crepe with some of the cheese mixture and fold over. Place in a buttered shallow baking dish.
10. Dot with the ¼ cup butter and bake in a 350°F (180°C) oven for 20-30 minutes.
11. Sprinkle with chopped parsley and serve immediately.

Serves 6.

# Lebanese Crepes

18 crepes
½ cup (125 ml) olive oil
3 cloves garlic, minced
5 medium onions, chopped
2 lb (1 kg) boned lamb, cubed
4 cups chopped tomatoes

1½ cups (375 ml) tomato juice
2 teaspoons thyme
½ teaspoon cinnamon
1 lb (500 g) diced eggplant
4 tablespoons raisins
4 tablespoons pine nuts

1. Make the crepes using the Basic Crepe Batter recipe (see Index). Set aside.
2. Sauté the garlic and onions in the olive oil until the onions are transparent.
3. Add the lamb and cook, stirring frequently, until the lamb is well-browned on all sides.
4. Stir in the tomatoes, tomato juice, thyme and cinnamon, cover and cook until the lamb is tender.
5. Add the eggplant, raisins and pine nuts and cook until the eggplant is soft.
6. Remove the cover and boil rapidly until the liquid is reduced by half.
7. Fill each crepe with some of the lamb mixture. Fold over and place in a buttered shallow baking dish.
8. Bake in a 350°F (180°C) oven for 15 minutes. Serves 6.

# Egg and Bacon Crepes

18 crepes
½ lb (250 g) bacon
1 medium onion, minced
⅓ cup (85 g) butter

18 eggs
1 teaspoon salt
½ teaspoon black pepper
chopped parsley

1. Make the crepes using the Rich Crepe Batter recipe (see Index). Set aside and keep warm.
2. Cut the bacon into small pieces and cook in a large frypan until crisp. Remove from frypan and drain on absorbent paper.
3. Melt the butter in the same frypan and cook the onion until golden brown. Remove the onion from the frypan with a slotted spoon.
4. Lightly beat the eggs with the salt and pepper and cook in the frypan.
5. Mix in the bacon and onion.
6. Fill each crepe with some of the egg and bacon filling. Fold over and serve immediately, garnished with parsley. Serves 6.

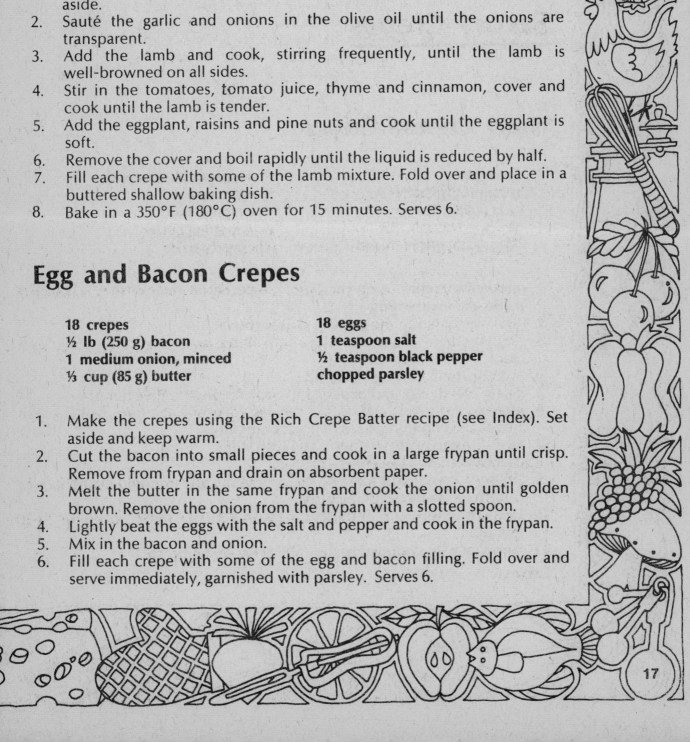

# Camembert Crepes

| | |
|---|---|
| 18 crepes | 1 teaspoon salt |
| ⅓ cup (85 g) butter | ½ teaspoon black pepper |
| ⅓ cup plain flour | 1½ lb (750 g) Camembert |
| 3 cups (750 ml) milk | ⅔ cup grated Cheddar cheese |

1. Make the crepes using the Basic Crepe Batter recipe (see Index). Set aside and keep warm.
2. Melt the butter in a saucepan. Remove from heat and stir in the flour. Return to a low heat and cook for three minutes. Slowly add the milk, stirring constantly. Add the salt and pepper and cook until thickened.
3. Cut the Camembert into chunks and place in a saucepan with half the sauce. Gently heat until the cheese begins to melt.
4. Fill each crepe with some of the cheese mixture. Fold over and place in a buttered shallow baking dish.
5. Pour on the remaining sauce, sprinkle with the grated cheese, and bake in a 350°F (180°C) oven for 20 minutes.

Serves 6.

# Tomato and Bacon Crepes

| | |
|---|---|
| 18 crepes | 1 teaspoon salt |
| 1 lb (500 g) bacon | ¼ teaspoon cayenne pepper |
| ½ cup plain flour | 8 medium tomatoes, diced |
| 2 cups grated Cheddar cheese | ½ cup chopped parsley |
| ½ cup (125 ml) dry sherry | |

1. Make the crepes using the Basic Crepe Batter recipe (see Index). Set aside.
2. Cut the bacon into small bits and cook until crisp. Remove from the pan with a slotted spoon and drain on absorbent paper. Reserve the bacon fat.
3. Blend ½ cup of the bacon fat with the flour in a saucepan.
4. Add ⅔ of the cheese, sherry, salt and pepper. Mix well. Cook until thick.
5. Mix the tomatoes and bacon into the cheese sauce.
6. Fill each crepe with the tomato mixture and either serve at once garnished with chopped parsley and remaining cheese or sprinkle on the rest of the cheese and heat in a 350°F (180°C) oven and then add the chopped parsley before serving.

Serves 6.

# Egg and Nut Crepes

18 crepes
1 cup (250 g) mayonnaise
1½ teaspoons salt
1 teaspoon coriander
¼ teaspoon black pepper
⅛ teaspoon paprika
½ teaspoon dry mustard
10 hard-boiled eggs, chopped
1 cup chopped nuts
1 cup chopped celery
2 scallions, minced

Sauce:
3 tablespoons (45 g) butter
2 tablespoons plain flour
1 teaspoon dry mustard
½ teaspoon salt
⅛ teaspoon cayenne pepper
½ teaspoon paprika
2 cups (500 ml) milk
1 cup grated Cheddar cheese

1. Make the crepes using the Basic Crepe Batter or Cheesey Crepe Batter recipe (see Index). Set aside.
2. Mix together the mayonnaise, salt, coriander, pepper, paprika and mustard in an electric blender.
3. Pour the mayonnaise mixture on the chopped eggs and mix with the nuts, celery and scallions.
4. Fill each crepe with the egg and nut filling. Fold over and place in a buttered shallow baking dish.
5. Melt the butter in a saucepan. Remove from the heat and stir in the flour until smooth. Return to a low heat and cook for two minutes.
6. Add the mustard, salt, cayenne pepper and paprika. Mix well.
7. Slowly add the milk, stirring constantly. Cook until thickened. Remove from heat.
8. Add the cheese and stir until the cheese is melted.
9. Pour the sauce over the crepes and bake in a 350°F (180°C) oven for 15 minutes.

Serves 6.

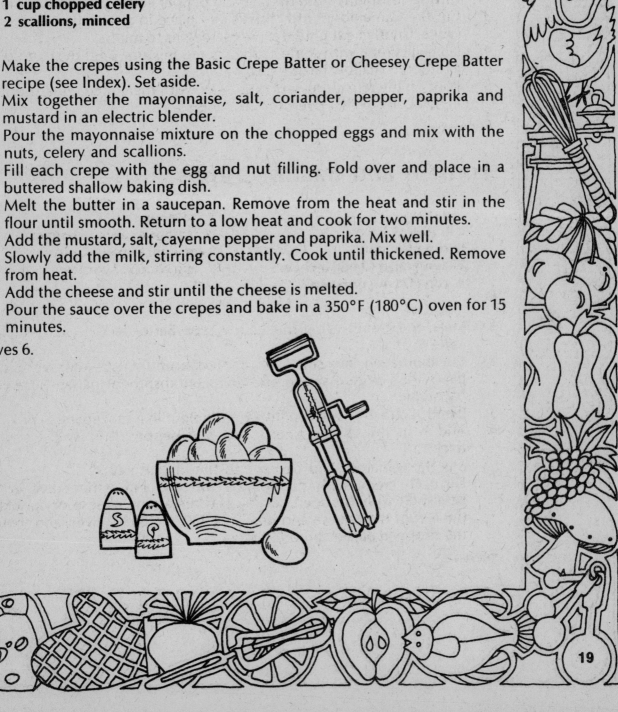

# Potato Curry Crepes

18 crepes
6 cups mashed potatoes
3 eggs
¼ cup (65 g) butter
¼ cup plain flour
1½ teaspoons curry powder

1½ cups (375 ml) milk
1 cup grated Cheddar cheese
1 teaspoon salt
¼ teaspoon cayenne pepper
butter for frying
chopped chives

1. Make the crepes using the Basic Crepe Batter or the Herb Crepe Batter recipe (see Index). Set aside.
2. Beat the eggs into the mashed potatoes one at a time. Set aside.
3. Melt the butter in a small saucepan. Remove from heat and stir in the flour and curry powder until smooth. Return to a low heat and cook for three minutes.
4. Slowly add the milk, cheese, salt and pepper, stirring constantly. Cook until thickened.
5. Pour the sauce into the potato mixture and blend well.
6. Fill each crepe with some of the mixture and fold over.
7. Heat butter in a large frypan and fry the crepes on both sides until golden brown.
8. Serve garnished with chopped chives.

Serves 6.

# Summer Squash Crepes

18 crepes
3 cups mashed summer
  squash
2 tablespoons butter

1½ tablespoons maple syrup or
  golden syrup
18 cooked breakfast sausages
nutmeg

1. Make the Crepes using the Basic Crepe Batter recipe (see Index). Set aside.
2. Combine the squash, butter, and syrup.
3. Spread each crepe with some of the mixture.
4. Place a sausage on each crepe and roll up. Place in a buttered shallow baking dish.
5. Sprinkle on a little nutmeg and bake in a 350°F (180°C) oven for 20 minutes.

Serves 6.

# Salmon Crepes with Lemon Sauce

18 crepes
2 lb (1 kg) canned salmon
1 medium onion, chopped
1 cup chopped celery
2 hard-boiled eggs, chopped
1 cup chopped fresh mushrooms
1 teaspoon salt
¼ teaspoon black pepper

**Lemon Sauce:**
1 cup (250 ml) cream
¾ lb (375 g) cream cheese
⅔ cup (165 ml) lemon juice
⅔ cup (165 ml) melted butter
½ teaspoon salt
¼ teaspoon cayenne pepper
chopped parsley

1. Make the crepes using the Basic Crepe Batter recipe (see Index). Set aside.
2. Drain the salmon and break up.
3. Mix the salmon with the onion, celery, eggs, mushrooms, salt and pepper. Set aside.
4. In the top of a double boiler whip the cream.
5. Place over simmering water and add the diced cream cheese, lemon juice, butter, salt and cayenne pepper. Stir until smooth and thick.
6. Pour about ⅔ of the sauce into the salmon mixture.
7. Fill the crepes with the salmon mixture. Fold over and place in a buttered shallow baking dish.
8. Pour on the remaining sauce and bake in a 350°F (180°C) oven for about 20 minutes.
9. Serve immediately sprinkled with chopped parsley.

Serves 6.

# Bacon and Bean Crepes

18 crepes
1 lb (500 g) bacon
½ cup plain flour
1½ cups (375 ml) milk
⅓ cup (85 ml) vinegar
2½ tablespoons sugar

1 teaspoon salt
¼ teaspoon black pepper
6 cups cooked, cut green beans
½ cup chopped parsley
3 hard-boiled eggs, chopped
chopped chives

1. Make the crepes using the Basic Crepe Batter or Beer Crepe Batter recipe (see Index). Set aside.
2. Chop up the bacon and cook in a large frypan until crisp.
3. Remove ⅓ of the bacon with a slotted spoon and drain on absorbent paper.
4. Remove the pan from the heat and stir in the flour.
5. Return to a low heat and add the milk, stirring constantly. Cook until thickened.
6. Add the vinegar, sugar, salt and pepper and blend thoroughly.
7. Mix together the green beans, parsley and chopped eggs.
8. Pour the sauce over the bean mixture and mix well.
9. Fill each crepe with the bean mixture and fold over.
10. Place in a buttered shallow baking dish and bake in a 350°F (180°C) oven for about 20 minutes.
11. Serve garnished with the remaining bacon and chopped chives. Serves 6.

# Salmon Crepes

18 crepes
2 lb (1 kg) canned salmon
1 cup (250 g) mayonnaise
½ cup relish
2½ tablespoons chopped parsley

2½ tablespoons chopped scallions
4 hard-boiled eggs, chopped
1 teaspoon salt
½ teaspoon black pepper

1. Make the crepes using the Basic Crepe Batter recipe (see Index). Set aside.
2. Drain and break up the salmon.
3. Mix the salmon with the mayonnaise, relish, parsley, scallions, eggs, salt and pepper.
4. Fill each crepe with some of the salmon filling. Fold over and place in a buttered shallow baking dish.
5. Bake in a 350°F (180°C) oven for 20 minutes. Serves 6.

# Spinach Crepes with Sour Cream Sauce

18 crepes
**Sour Cream Sauce:**
½ cup (125 g) butter
½ cup plain flour
1½ cups (375 ml) milk
2 cups (500 g) sour cream
1 teaspoon salt
¼ teaspoon black pepper

**Filling:**
3 lb (1½ kg) spinach
½ cup (125 g) butter
⅓ cup grated Parmesan cheese
⅓ cup chopped parsley
1¼ tablespoons minced chives
salt and pepper
4 egg yolks

1. Make the crepes using the Spinach Crepe Batter or Basic Crepe Batter recipe (see Index). Set aside and keep warm.
2. Melt the butter in a saucepan. Remove from heat and stir in the flour until smooth. Return to a low heat and cook for three minutes.
3. Gradually add the milk, sour cream, salt and pepper, stirring constantly. Cook until thickened. Set aside.
4. Remove the white center stem from the spinach and wash several times in cold water.
5. Cook the spinach in a large covered saucepan with no extra water added until the spinach is just cooked. Drain any excess water. Press the spinach through a sieve or purée in an electric blender.
6. Melt the butter in a saucepan and cook the spinach for two minutes over a low heat.
7. Add the Parmesan cheese, parsley and chives.
8. Season to taste with salt and pepper. Remove from heat.
9. Add the egg yolks one at a time beating well after each addition.
10. Fill each crepe with the spinach mixture. Fold over and place in a buttered shallow baking dish.
11. Pour the Sour Cream Sauce over the crepes and bake in a 350°F (180°C) oven for about 20 minutes or until heated through. Serves 6.

# Broccoli Crepes with Cream Sauce

18 crepes
Cream Sauce:
5 tablespoons (100 g) butter
5 tablespoons plain flour
3½ cups (875 ml) cream
¾ teaspoon salt
¼ teaspoon black pepper

Filling:
4 cups chopped broccoli
    flowerets
¾ cup (185 g) butter
1 teaspoon grated lemon rind
1 cup slivered almonds

1. Make the crepes using the Lemon Crepe Batter recipe omitting the sugar (see Index). Set aside and keep warm.
2. Melt the butter in a saucepan. Remove from the heat and stir in the flour until smooth. Return to a low heat and cook for five minutes. Gradually stir in the cream, salt and pepper. Cook until thickened. Do not allow to boil. Set aside.
3. Sauté the broccoli in half the butter and lemon rind over a low heat for about 15 minutes or until the broccoli is tender. Remove from heat.
4. Add half the sauce and half the almonds to the broccoli and blend thoroughly.
5. Fill the crepes with the broccoli mixture. Fold over and place in a buttered shallow baking dish.
6. Dot with the remaining butter. Pour over the rest of the sauce and sprinkle on the remaining almonds.
7. Bake in a 350°F (180°C) oven for about 20 minutes. Serves 6.

# Chicken and Ham Crepes

18 crepes
4 cups chopped cooked chicken
1 cup chopped ham
1½ cups diced Mozzarella cheese

½ cup chopped chives
3 cups (750 ml) sour cream
1 teaspoon salt
¼ cup (65 g) butter

1. Make the crepes using the Beer Crepe Batter recipe (see Index). Set aside and keep warm.
2. Mix together the chicken, ham, half the cheese, the chives, sour cream and salt.
3. Fill each crepe with some of the chicken and ham filling. Fold over and place in a buttered shallow baking dish.
4. Sprinkle on the remaining cheese and dot with the butter.
5. Bake in a 350°F (180°C) oven for ½ hour. Serves 6.

# Mushroom Crepes with Cream Sauce

18 crepes
Cheese Sauce:
½ cup (125 g) butter
½ cup plain flour
1 teaspoon salt
¼ teaspoon black pepper
4 cups (1 quart) cream

⅔ cup grated Parmesan cheese

Filling:
4 cups sliced mushrooms
¾ cup (185 g) butter
salt and pepper

1. Make the crepes using the Basic Crepe Batter recipe (see Index). Set aside and keep warm.
2. Melt the butter in a saucepan. Remove from the heat and stir in the flour, salt and pepper until smooth. Return to a low heat and cook for five minutes.
3. Slowly pour in the cream, stirring constantly. Cook until thickened. Do not boil.
4. Add the cheese and stir until the cheese has melted and the sauce is smooth and creamy.
5. Sauté the mushrooms in half the butter for about five minutes.
6. Pour in half the Cheese Sauce and salt and pepper to taste. Mix well.
7. Fill each crepe with the mushroom filling. Fold over and place in a buttered shallow baking dish. Dot with the remaining butter and pour on the rest of the sauce.
8. Bake in a 350°F (180°C) oven for ½ hour. Serves 6.

# Ham and Banana Crepes

18 crepes
2 lb (1 kg) cooked ham, cubed
6 bananas, peeled and diced
¼ cup (65 g) butter

1 teaspoon dry mustard
1½ cups grated Cheddar cheese
salt and pepper

1. Make the crepes using the Basic Crepe Batter recipe (see Index). Set aside.
2. Sauté the ham and bananas in the butter until heated through.
3. Stir in the mustard, cheese and salt and pepper to taste.
4. Fill each crepe with the ham and banana mixture. Fold over and place in a buttered shallow baking dish.
5. Bake in a 350°F (180°C) oven for ten minutes. Serves 6.

# Asparagus Crepes

18 crepes
1½ lb (750 g) fresh asparagus
½ cup (125 g) butter
1 teaspoon salt
¼ teaspoon black pepper

Hollandaise Sauce:
8 egg yolks
¼ cup (65 ml) water
1⅓ cups (335 g) butter
3 tablespoons lemon juice
salt and pepper

1.  Make the crepes using the Herb Crepe Batter recipe (see Index). Set aside and keep warm.
2.  Wash the asparagus very well several times in cold water. Cut into small pieces.
3.  Melt the butter and cook the asparagus over a low heat until tender. Sprinkle with salt and pepper. Set aside and keep warm.
4.  Beat egg yolks in top of a double boiler. Add water, beat again.
5.  Place on top of simmering water and add the butter a little at a time, beating well after each addition. Beat until the sauce is thick. Remove from heat.
6.  Add the lemon juice and salt and pepper to taste.
7.  Fill each crepe with the cooked asparagus. Fold over and place in a buttered shallow baking dish.
8.  Bake in a 350°F (180°C) oven for about 20 minutes or until heated.
9.  Pour on the Hollandaise Sauce and serve immediately.

Serves 6.

# Chicken with Asparagus Crepes

18 crepes
4 cups chopped cooked chicken
2½ cups chopped cooked asparagus
1½ cups grated Cheddar cheese

⅔ cup (165 ml) lemon juice
½ cup chopped parsley
1 teaspoon salt
½ teaspoon black pepper
½ cup (125 g) butter

1.  Make the crepes using the Cheesey Crepe Batter recipe (see Index). Set aside and keep warm.
2.  Mix together the chicken, asparagus, cheese, lemon juice, parsley, salt and pepper.
3.  Fill each crepe with some of the chicken filling. Fold over and place in a buttered shallow baking dish.
4.  Dot with the butter and bake in a 350°F (180°C) oven for ½ hour.

Serves 6.

# Paprika Veal Crepes

18 crepes
2 lb (1 kg) boned veal
1½ teaspoons salt
½ teaspoon black pepper
1½ tablespoons paprika
3 small onions, chopped
2 cloves garlic, minced
⅔ cup (165 g) butter

3 tablespoons plain flour
2 cups (500 ml) chicken stock
1 cup chopped tomatoes
½ cup chopped red pepper
1 teaspoon Tabasco sauce
1 cup (250 g) sour cream
4 tablespoons chopped chives

1. Make the crepes using the Basic Crepe Batter recipe (see Index). Set aside and keep warm.
2. Cut the veal into small cubes.
3. Mix together the salt, pepper and paprika. Sprinkle on the veal and mix well to ensure that the cubes are all coated.
4. Sauté the onions and garlic in half the butter until the onions are transparent.
5. Add the veal and brown well over a medium heat.
6. Sprinkle the flour over the meat, then stir in the chicken stock.
7. Add the tomatoes, pepper and Tabasco sauce to the meat mixture. Cover and gently simmer for about 45 minutes or until the meat is tender. Remove from the heat.
8. Stir in the sour cream.
9. Fill each crepe with some of the veal filling. Fold over and place in a buttered baking dish.
10. Dot with the remaining butter and bake in a 350°F (180°C) oven for about ½ hour. Sprinkle with chopped chives and serve immediately.

Serves 6.

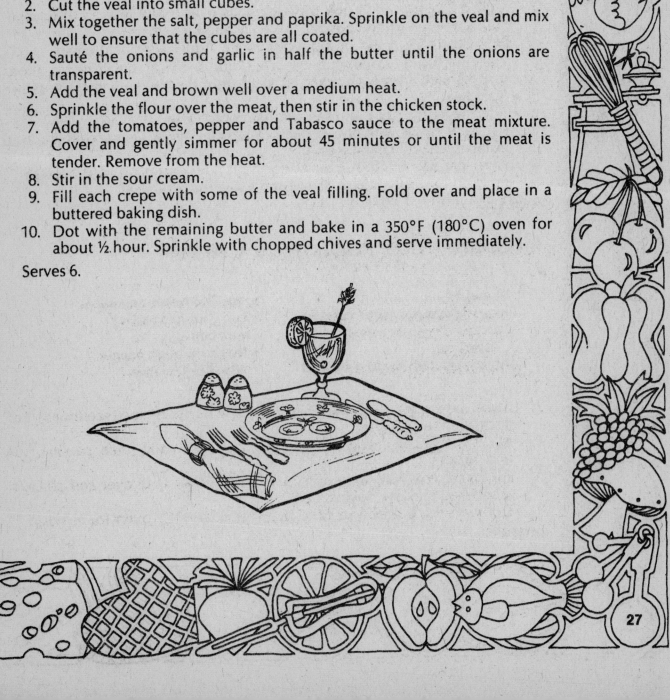

# Welsh Rarebit Crepes

12 crepes
1½ tablespoons cornstarch
3 cups grated Cheddar
  cheese
1 cup (250 ml) milk
1½ teaspoons dry mustard

2 teaspoons Worcestershire
  sauce
2 eggs, beaten
1 cup cooked bacon bits
1 cup chopped tomatoes
½ cup chopped parsley

1. Make the crepes using the Basic Crepe Batter recipe (see Index). Set aside.
2. Mix together the cornstarch and cheese in a saucepan.
3. Add the milk, dry mustard, Worcestershire sauce and eggs. Mix well.
4. Cook over a low heat until the cheese melts, stirring constantly.
5. Add half the bacon bits to the cheese mixture.
6. Fill the crepes with ⅔ of the mixture and fold over.
7. Place in a buttered shallow baking dish and spoon on the chopped tomatoes. Pour on the remaining sauce.
8. Bake in a 350°F (180°C) oven for 20 minutes.
9. Sprinkle with the chopped parsley and remaining bacon bits. Serve immediately.

Serves 4.

# Zucchini Crepes

18 crepes
4 tablespoons (60 g) butter
4 tablespoons olive oil
3 cloves garlic, minced
2 lb (1 kg) zucchini

1½ cups chopped tomatoes
1 teaspoon salt
½ teaspoon black pepper
⅓ cup dry bread crumbs

1. Make the crepes using the Herb Crepe Batter or Basic Crepe Batter recipe (see Index). Set aside and keep warm.
2. Melt the butter with the olive oil in a large frypan and sauté the garlic for two minutes over a low heat.
3. Slice the zucchini and add to the garlic with the tomatoes, salt and pepper. Cook over a low heat for ten minutes.
4. Stir in the bread crumbs and mix thoroughly.
5. Fill each crepe with the zucchini filling. Fold over and serve immediately.

Serves 6.

# Curried Lamb Crepes

18 crepes
3 small onions, chopped
3 cloves garlic, minced
½ teaspoon crushed bay leaves
1 red pepper, chopped
⅔ cup (165 g) butter
2 lb (1 kg) boned lamb
½ cup (125 ml) lemon juice

1 teaspoon salt
½ teaspoon black pepper
⅓ cup plain flour
curry powder to taste
1 cup (250 ml) cream
3 cups (750 ml) milk
⅔ cup desiccated coconut

1. Make the crepes using the Basic Crepe Batter recipe (see Index). Set aside and keep warm.
2. Sauté the onions, garlic, bay leaves and pepper in half the butter until the onions are transparent.
3. Add the meat and brown well, stirring constantly. Reduce the heat and cook until the meat is tender. Remove from the heat.
4. Stir in the lemon juice, salt and pepper. Set aside.
5. Melt the remaining butter in a saucepan. Remove from the heat and stir in the flour and curry powder. When smooth return to the heat and cook over a low heat for five minutes.
6. Slowly add the cream and milk, stirring constantly. Cook until thickened.
7. Add the lamb mixture to the sauce and mix thoroughly. Cook until heated through.
8. Fill each crepe with the filling. Fold over and place in a buttered shallow baking dish.
9. Bake in a 350°F (180°C) oven for about 20 minutes.
10. Serve immediately with desiccated coconut.

Serves 6.

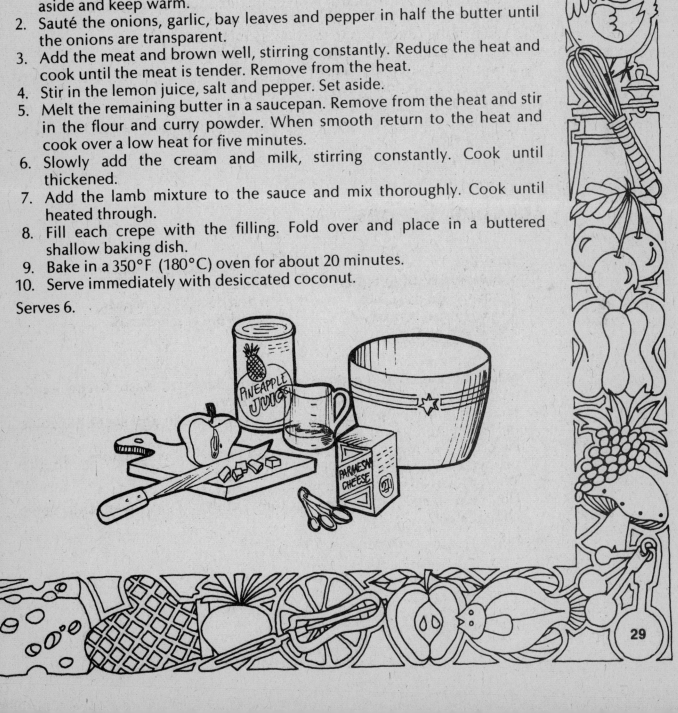

# Spanish Crepes

18 crepes
⅓ cup (85 g) butter
2 cloves garlic, minced
1 cup chopped ham
18 eggs, beaten
¼ cup chopped parsley
1 tablespoon chopped chives

Sauce:
1½ lb (750 g) tinned tomatoes
2 small onions, chopped
2 cloves garlic, minced
2½ tablespoons olive oil
½ teaspoon salt
¼ teaspoon black pepper

1.  Make the crepes using the Basic Crepe Batter or Herb Crepe Batter recipe (see Index). Set aside.
2.  Melt the butter in a large frypan and sauté the garlic, onions, green pepper and ham until the onions are soft.
3.  Mix the eggs with the parsley and chives, then add to the frypan and cook until the eggs are cooked but still wet.
4.  Fill each crepe with the egg mixture. Fold over and place in a buttered shallow baking dish.
5.  Drain the tomatoes but reserve the juice. Chop the tomatoes coarsely.
6.  Sauté the tomatoes, onions, celery, pepper and garlic in the olive oil for five minutes.
7.  Add the salt and pepper and the reserved tomato juice. Mix well and cook over a medium heat until the liquid is reduced by half.
8.  Pour the sauce over the crepes and bake in a 350°F (180°C) oven for 15 minutes.

Serves 6.

# Frankfurter Crepes

12 crepes
12 frankfurters
3 cups sauerkraut
2 cups grated Swiss cheese

1.  Make the crepes using the Basic Crepe Batter recipe (see Index). Set aside.
2.  Gently cook the frankfurters with the sauerkraut until heated through.
3.  Put one frankfurter on each crepe and top with the sauerkraut. Fold over and place in a buttered shallow baking dish.
4.  Sprinkle on the grated Swiss cheese and bake in a 350°F (180°C) oven for about 15 minutes or until the cheese has melted.

Serves 4-6.

# Lamb Crepes with Wine Sauce

18 crepes
**Wine Sauce:**
¾ cup (185 g) butter
¾ cup plain flour
3 cups (750 ml) beef stock
1¼ cups (300 ml) red wine
1 teaspoon salt
¼ teaspoon black pepper
¼ cup chopped fresh tarragon

**Filling:**
2 small onions, chopped
3 cloves garlic, minced
⅔ cup (165 ml) butter
1 cup chopped tomatoes
½ cup (125 ml) red wine
2 lb (1 kg) boneless lamb, cut into cubes
1 teaspoon salt

1. Make the crepes using the Herb Crepe Batter or Basic Crepe Batter recipe (see Index). Set aside and keep warm.
2. Melt the butter in a saucepan. Remove from heat and stir in the flour until smooth. Return to the heat and cook over a low heat for five minutes.
3. Gradually add the beef stock and red wine, stirring constantly. Cook until thickened.
4. Add the salt, pepper and tarragon and simmer for five minutes. Set aside.
5. Sauté the onions and garlic in half the butter until the onions are transparent.
6. Add the tomatoes and red wine and cook until the liquid is reduced.
7. Stir in the lamb and cook for about 20 minutes, stirring frequently.
8. Add the salt and cook until the meat is tender.
9. Pour half the sauce into the lamb mixture. Stir well.
10. Fill the crepes with the filling and fold over. Place in a buttered shallow baking dish. Dot with the remaining butter and pour on the rest of the sauce.
11. Bake in a 375°F (190°C) oven for about 20 minutes.

Serves 6.

# Mixed Vegetable Crepes

18 crepes
2 cloves garlic, minced
2 small onions, chopped
½ cup (125 g) butter
4 zucchinis, sliced
2 cups chopped tomatoes
1 medium eggplant, peeled and
  diced

1 green pepper, chopped
1 red pepper, chopped
⅓ cup chopped parsley
½ teaspoon crushed bay leaves
½ teaspoon basil
1 teaspoon salt
½ teaspoon black pepper
⅔ cup grated cheese

1. Make the crepes using the Basic Crepe Batter recipe (see Index). Set aside and keep warm.
2. Sauté the garlic and onions in the butter until the onions are golden brown.
3. Add the zucchinis, tomatoes, eggplant, green and red peppers, parsley, bay leaves, basil, salt and pepper.
4. Cover and cook over a low heat for ten minutes. Remove the cover and simmer until all the liquid evaporates.
5. Fill each crepe with some of the mixture. Fold over and serve immediately sprinkled with grated cheese. Serves 6.

# Avocado and Ham Crepes

18 crepes
3 medium avocados
1 teaspoon salt
¼ teaspoon black pepper
⅔ cup (165 g) butter, melted

4 cups chopped ham
¾ cup (185 ml) dry sherry
2 cups (500 ml) cream
1 tablespoon prepared French
  mustard

1. Make the crepes using the Basic Crepe Batter recipe (see Index). Set aside and keep warm.
2. Remove the flesh from the avocados. Chop and purée in an electric blender with the salt, pepper and half the melted butter. Set aside.
3. Mix together the ham, sherry, cream and mustard in a saucepan. Bring to a boil. Remove from heat.
4. Spread each crepe with the avocado mixture, then top with the ham mixture. Fold over and place in a buttered shallow baking dish.
5. Pour on the remaining melted butter and bake in a 350°F (180°C) oven for about ½ hour. Serves 6.

# Veal Crepes with Mornay Sauce

**18 crepes**
**Mornay Sauce:**
½ cup (125 g) butter
½ cup plain flour
2 cups (500 ml) chicken stock
1 cup (250 ml) cream
3 egg yolks
¾ cup grated Parmesan cheese
1 teaspoon salt
½ teaspoon black pepper

**Filling:**
2 lb (1 kg) stewing veal
1¼ cups (300 ml) chicken stock
½ cup (125 ml) dry white wine
⅔ cup (165 g) butter
2 small onions, chopped
¼ cup chopped parsley
1¼ tablespoons chopped chives
1 teaspoon salt
¼ teaspoon black pepper

1. Make the crepes using the Herb Crepe Batter recipe (see Index). Set aside and keep warm.
2. Melt the butter in the top of a double boiler. Add the flour and mix until smooth. Cook for five minutes.
3. Gradually pour on the stock, stirring constantly. Remove from heat.
4. Add the cream and the egg yolks one at a time, beating well after each addition. Return to the heat.
5. Add the Parmesan cheese, salt and pepper and cook, stirring constantly, until thick and creamy. Set aside and keep just warm.
6. Dice the veal and simmer in the chicken stock and white wine until tender. Set aside.
7. Sauté the onions in half the butter until transparent.
8. Add the veal and simmer for five minutes.
9. Remove from the heat and stir in the parsley, chives, salt and pepper and half the Mornay Sauce.
10. Fill each crepe with the veal filling and fold over. Place in a buttered shallow baking dish. Dot with the remaining butter and pour on the rest of the sauce.
11. Bake in a 350°F (180°C) oven for ½ hour. Serves 6.

# Shrimp Crepes with Tomato Sauce

18 crepes
Tomato Sauce:
½b cup (125 ml) olive oil
4 medium onions, chopped
½ cup chopped celery
3 cloves garlic, minced
2 bay leaves
1 teaspoon oregano
½ teaspoon thyme
½ teaspoon basil
⅓ cup chopped parsley
1 teaspoon salt
½ teaspoon black pepper
3 cups chopped tomatoes

⅔ cup (165 g) tomato paste
¼ cup (65 g) butter

Filling:
2 medium onions, chopped
½ cup (125 g) butter
½ cup (125 ml) dry white wine
3 lb (1½ kg) shrimps
4 tablespoons tomato paste
1½ tablespoons lemon juice
⅓ cup chopped parsley
1 teaspoon salt
½ teaspoon black pepper
⅔ cup grated Parmesan cheese

1. Make the crepes using the Spinach Crepe Batter recipe (see Index). Set aside and keep warm.
2. Make the Tomato Sauce by heating the olive oil in a large saucepan. Sauté the onions until transparent.
3. Add the celery and garlic and cook until the onions are golden brown.
4. Add the remaining Sauce ingredients except the butter and cook over a low heat for ½ hour.
5. Press through a sieve or purée in an electric blender.
6. Return to the saucepan and simmer for five minutes.
7. Stir the butter in until it is melted. Set aside.
8. Sauté the onions in the butter until transparent.

9. Add the wine and bring to a boil. Boil rapidly until the liquid is reduce to half.

10. Peel and de-vein the shrimps and chop coarsely. Add to the onions and cook for about five minutes, stirring constantly. Remove from heat.
11. Stir in the tomato paste, lemon juice, parsley, salt, pepper and half the Tomato Sauce.
12. Fill each crepe with some of the Filling and fold over. Place in a buttered shallow baking dish.
13. Pour the remaining Sauce over the crepes and sprinkle with the grated Parmesan cheese.
14. Bake in a 375°F (190°C) oven for about ½ hour.

Serves 6.

# Scallops in Wine Sauce

18 crepes
Wine Sauce:
¾ cup (185 g) butter
¾ cup plain flour
2½ cups (625 ml) chicken stock
1½ cups (375 ml) dry white wine
1 teaspoon salt
½ teaspoon black pepper
1½ tablespoons minced
   parsley

Filling:
⅓ cup (85 g) butter
1 medium onion, minced
1 clove garlic, minced
⅔ cup (165 ml) dry white wine
2 lb (1 kg) scallops, chopped
½ cup chopped parsley
1 teaspoon salt
¼ teaspoon black pepper
chopped chives

1. Make the crepes using the Basic Crepe Batter Recipe (see Index). Set aside and keep warm.
2. Make the Wine Sauce by melting the butter in a saucepan. Remove from the heat and stir in the flour until smooth. Return to the heat and cook over a low heat for four minutes.
3. Slowly add the chicken stock, stirring constantly.
4. Add the white wine, salt, pepper and minced parsley. Blend thoroughly. Set aside.
5. Melt the ⅓ cup butter in a large frypan and sauté the onion and garlic until the onion is transparent.
6. Add the wine and bring to a boil. Boil rapidly until the liquid is reduced to ⅓ cup.
7. Add the scallops and cook over a medium heat, stirring frequently, for ten minutes.
8. Add the parsley, salt and pepper and cook for another five minutes.
9. Add half the sauce and heat thoroughly.
10. Fill each crepe with some of the filling. Fold over and place in a buttered shallow baking dish.
11. Pour the remaining sauce over the crepes and bake in a 375°F (190°C) oven for about 20 minutes.
12. Serve sprinkled with chopped chives.

Serves 6.

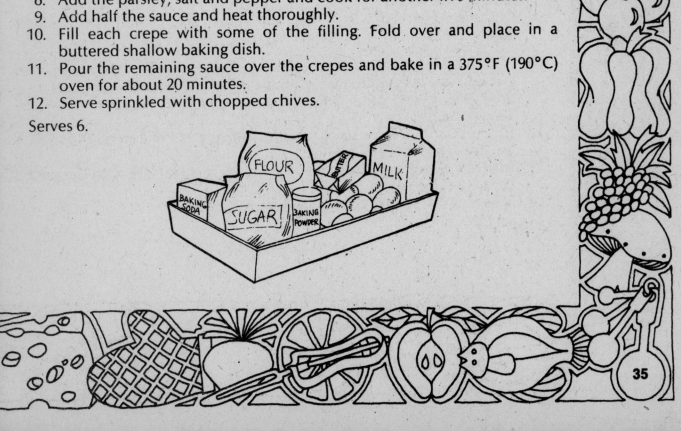

# Crab Crepes with Bearnaise Sauce

18 crepes
Bearnaise Sauce:
½ cup (125 ml) tarragon
  vinegar
5 scallions, minced
1 tablespoon minced fresh
  tarragon
10 white peppercorns,
  crushed
5 egg yolks
¼ cup (65 ml) boiling water
1 cup (250 g) butter

Filling:
4 scallions, chopped
½ cup chopped green pepper
⅓ cup (85 g) butter
½ cup (125 ml) dry white wine
4 cups cooked, chopped
  crabmeat
½ cup dry bread crumbs
¼ cup (65 ml) lemon juice
½ cup chopped parsley
1 teaspoon salt
½ teaspoon black pepper

1. Make the crepes using the Basic Crepe Batter recipe (see Index). Set aside and keep warm.
2. Make the Bearnaise Sauce by combining the vinegar, scallions, tarragon and peppercorns in a saucepan. Bring to a boil and cook until reduced to three tablespoons. Strain through a fine sieve. Pour into the top of a double boiler.
3. Add the egg yolks, one at a time, beating well after each addition.
4. Add the boiling water, beating constantly. Put the pan over slightly simmering water and beat until smooth and creamy. Remove from the heat.
5. Add the butter a little at a time. Beat after each addition until melted and smooth. Put the sauce over warm water to keep just warm until ready to use.
6. Sauté the scallions and green pepper in the butter in a medium saucepan. Cook for two minutes.
7. Stir in the wine and boil rapidly for one minute.
8. Stir in the crabmeat and cook over a low heat for three minutes.
9. Add the bread crumbs, lemon juice, parsley, salt and pepper and blend thoroughly. Cook until well-heated.
10. Fill each crepe with some of the crabmeat filling and fold over. Place on a serving dish and pour on the Bearnaise Sauce.

Serves 6.

# Fish Crepes with Sherry Sauce

18 crepes
Sherry Sauce:
⅓ cup (85 g) butter
⅓ cup plain flour
½ teaspoon salt
¼ teaspoon black pepper
3 cups (750 ml) cream
½ cup (125 ml) dry sherry
Filling:
750 g (1½ lb) white fish fillets

¾ cup (185 g) butter
2 cups (500 ml) chicken stock
2 small onions, chopped
¼ lb (125 g) fresh mushrooms
4 tablespoons chopped parsley
1 teaspoon salt
¼ teaspoon black pepper
½ cup grated Parmesan cheese

1. Make the crepes using the Basic Crepe Batter recipe (see Index).
2. Melt the butter in a saucepan. Remove from the heat and stir in the flour, salt and pepper. Stir until smooth. Return to a low heat and cook for three minutes.
3. Gradually add the cream, stirring constantly, and cook until thick.
4. Add the sherry and mix well. Set aside.
5. Gently fry the fish fillets in half the butter for five minutes.
6. Pour on the chicken stock and simmer for five minutes. Remove the fish from the pan. Set aside.
7. Sauté the onions in the remaining butter until transparent.
8. Wipe the mushrooms with a damp cloth and slice. Add to onions and cook for five minutes.
9. Break up the fish fillets and add to the onion and mushroom mixture. Cook until heated through.
10. Stir half the white sherry sauce into the fish mixture with the parsley, salt and pepper.
11. Fill each crepe with some of the filling. Fold over and place in a shallow buttered baking dish. Pour on the rest of the sauce.
12. Sprinkle on the grated cheese and bake in a 375°F (190°C) oven for about 15 minutes.

Serves 6.

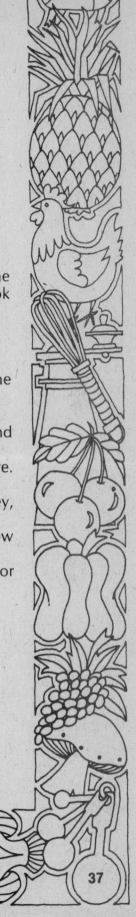

# Chinese Pork Crepes

18 crepes
1½ lb (750 g) pork fillets
2 teaspoons grated fresh ginger
¼ teaspoon dry mustard
1½ tablespoons brown sugar

½ teaspoon salt
⅔ cup (165 ml) soy sauce
⅓ cup (85 ml) vegetable oil
½ cup (125 ml) prepared sweet
and sour sauce

1. Make the crepes using the Basic Crepe Batter recipe (see Index). Set aside.
2. Cut the pork fillets into small cubes.
3. Mix together the ginger, mustard, brown sugar, salt and soy sauce.
4. Add the meat and mix thoroughly. Set aside and allow to marinate for about 45 minutes.
5. Drain well and sauté the meat in the vegetable oil until tender.
6. Add half the sweet and sour sauce to the pork and mix well.
7. Fill the crepes with the pork mixture and fold over. Place in a buttered shallow baking dish.
8. Mix together the marinade and the remaining sweet and sour sauce.
9. Pour over the crepes and bake in a 350°F (180°C) oven for 20 minutes.

Serves 6.

# Cheese Crepes

18 crepes
1 cup (250 g) butter
3 cups grated Cheddar cheese
1½ cups (375 ml) cream
2½ tablespoons chopped parsley
2½ tablespoons chopped chives

1. Make the crepes using the Cheesey Crepe Batter recipe (see Index). Set aside and keep warm.
2. Soften the butter and mix in the grated cheese.
3. Add the cream, parsley and chives and mix thoroughly.
4. Fill each crepe with some of the cheese filling. Fold over and place in a buttered shallow baking dish.
5. Bake in a 350°F (180°C) oven for about 20 minutes or until thoroughly heated.

Serves 6.

# Curried Shrimp Crepes

18 crepes
⅔ cup (165 g) butter
10 scallions, chopped
2 lb (1 kg) cooked shrimps
½ cup (125 ml) lemon juice
1 teaspoon salt

½ teaspoon black pepper
⅓ cup plain flour
curry powder to taste
1 cup (250 ml) cream
1 cup slivered almonds

1. Make the crepes using the Basic Crepe Batter recipe (see Index). Set aside and keep warm.
2. Melt half the butter in a saucepan and sauté the scallions for three minutes.
3. Peel and de-vein the shrimps. If large, chop coarsely. If small, leave whole.
4. Add the shrimps to the scallions and cook for five minutes.
5. Stir in the lemon juice, salt and pepper. Remove from heat and cover.
6. In another saucepan melt the remaining butter. Remove from heat and stir in the flour and curry powder. When smooth return to a low heat and cook for five minutes.
7. Slowly add the cream and milk to the butter and flour, stirring constantly. Cook until thickened.
8. Pour the white sauce over the shrimps and mix thoroughly. Heat well.
9. Fill the crepes with the shrimp mixture and fold over.
10. Serve immediately garnished with slivered almonds. Serves 6.

# Corned Beef Crepes

18 crepes
4 medium onions, cooked
4 medium carrots, cooked
4 cups chopped corned beef

1 cup cooked chopped cabbage
1 cup cooked diced potatoes
½ cup (125 ml) tomato sauce
salt and pepper

1. Make the crepes using the Basic Crepe Batter recipe (see Index). Set aside.
2. Mix together the onions, carrots, corned beef, cabbage, potatoes and tomato sauce.
3. Season to taste with salt and pepper.
4. Fill each crepe with some of the mixture. Fold over and place in a buttered shallow baking dish.
5. Bake in a 350°F (180°C) oven for 20 minutes. Serves 6.

39

# Tuna Fish Crepes with White Sauce

18 crepes
White Sauce:
⅓ cup (85 g) butter
⅓ cup plain flour
½ teaspoon salt
¼ teaspoon black pepper
3 cups (750 ml) cream
Filling:
½ cup (125 g) butter

2 small onions, chopped
1 clove garlic, minced
1 green pepper, chopped
4 cups drained canned tuna fish
1 teaspoon salt
½ teaspoon black pepper
4 hard-boiled eggs, chopped

1. Make the crepes using a crepe recipe of your choice. (see Index). Set aside and keep warm.
2. Melt the ⅓ cup butter in the top of a double boiler. Stir in the flour, salt and pepper and cook for about five minutes.
3. Add the cream and stir until smooth. Cook until thick, stirring constantly. Set aside.
4. Melt the half cup of butter in a saucepan and sauté the onions and garlic until the onions are transparent.
5. Add the green pepper and cook until the onions are golden brown.
6. Add the tuna fish and blend thoroughly. Heat through.
7. Stir in the salt and pepper and half the white sauce.
8. Fill each crepe with some of the filling and fold over.
9. Place the filled crepes in a shallow buttered baking dish.
10. Pour over the remaining sauce and bake in a 375°F (190°C) oven for about ½ hour.
11. Serve garnished with chopped eggs.

Serves 6.

# Lobster Crepes

12-18 crepes
⅓ cup (85 g) butter
⅔ cup cooked scallions
4 cups cooked chopped lobster
    meat
½ cup chopped parsley
1 teaspoon salt
½ teaspoon black pepper

**Bechamel Sauce:**
⅓ cup (85 g) butter
⅓ cup plain flour
1½ cups (375 ml) chicken stock
1 cup (250 ml) cream
½ teaspoon salt
¼ teaspoon black pepper
¼ cup (65 ml) dry sherry

1. Make the crepes using the Basic Crepe Batter Recipe (see Index) and keep warm.
2. Sauté the scallions in the butter for three minutes.
3. Add the lobster, parsley, salt and pepper. Blend thoroughly and remove from heat.
4. Make the sauce by melting the butter in a medium saucepan. Remove from heat.
5. Stir in the flour and mix until smooth. Return to heat and cook for five minutes.
6. Remove from heat and add the chicken stock. Mix thoroughly. Return to the heat and cook, stirring constantly, until thickened.
7. Add the cream, salt and pepper and blend thoroughly. Do not allow to boil.
8. Remove from the heat and stir in the dry sherry.
9. Stir about ⅔ of the sauce into the lobster mixture. Heat through.
10. Fill each crepe with some of the lobster mixture. Fold over and place on a serving platter or individual plates. Pour the remaining sauce over the crepes and serve.

Serves 6.

# Italian Chicken Crepes

18 crepes
1½ lb (750 g) boned raw chicken meat
⅓ cup (85 ml) olive oil
2 cloves garlic, minced
½ lb (250 g) fresh mushrooms
2 medium onions, chopped
1½ teaspoons oregano

1 teaspoon thyme
1½ lb (750 g) canned tomatoes
1 cup (250 ml) canned Italian tomato sauce
⅔ cup grated Parmesan cheese
1½ teaspoons salt
½ teaspoon black pepper
chopped parsley

1. Make the crepes using the Basic Crepe Batter or Wholemeal Crepe Batter recipe (see Index). Set aside.
2. Cut the chicken meat into small cubes.
3. Sauté the chicken in the olive oil with the garlic. Cook until the chicken loses its pinkness.
4. Wipe the mushrooms with a damp cloth and cut into fine slices.
5. Cook the mushrooms, onions, oregano and thyme with the chicken mixture.
6. Drain the tomatoes and chop coarsely.
7. Stir the chopped tomatoes into the chicken mixture with the tomato sauce, half the Parmesan cheese, the salt and pepper. Cook over a medium heat, uncovered, until the mixture is fairly dry.
8. Fill each crepe with the mixture. Fold over and place in a buttered shallow baking dish.
9. Sprinkle with the remaining Parmesan cheese and bake in a 350°F (180°C) oven for about 20 minutes.
10. Sprinkle with chopped parsley and serve immediately. Serves 6.

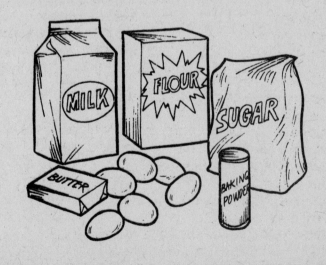

# Beef Crepes with Sour Cream Sauce

18 crepes
Filling:
3 tablespoons (45 g) butter
1 medium onion, chopped
2 lb (1 kg) ground beef
⅓ cup tomato paste
½ teaspoon nutmeg
¼ teaspoon cinnamon
⅓ cup (85 ml) olive oil

3 cloves garlic, minced
2 medium eggplants, peeled and diced
½ cup (125 ml) water
Sour Cream Sauce:
3 cups (750 g) sour cream
2 cloves garlic, minced
1 cup grated Parmesan cheese
2 eggs, beaten

1. Make the crepes using the Basic Crepe Batter or Beer Crepe Batter recipe (see Index). Set aside.
2. Melt the butter in a large saucepan and sauté the onion until transparent.
3. Add the beef, tomato paste, nutmeg and cinnamon. Cook, stirring frequently, until the beef is well-browned.
4. In a frypan heat the oil and sauté the garlic and eggplants for five minutes over a medium heat. Add the water and cook for ten minutes.
5. Mix the eggplant mixture with the meat mixture. Set aside.
6. Beat together the sour cream, garlic, Parmesan cheese and eggs.
7. Fill each crepe with the meat mixture and fold over. Place in a buttered shallow baking dish.
8. Pour on the sauce and bake in a 350°F (180°C) for 20 minutes. Serves 6.

# Veal Crepes

18 crepes
½ cup (125 g) butter
1 cup chopped onions
2 lb (1 kg) veal steak

2 teaspoons paprika
1½ teaspoons salt
⅓ cup (85 g) tomato paste
2 cups (500 g) sour cream

1. Make the crepes using the Basic Crepe Batter recipe (see Index). Set aside.
2. Sauté the onions in the butter until they are transparent.
3. Cut the veal into very thin slices and add to the onions with the paprika, salt and tomato paste. Cover and cook until the veal is tender.
4. Stir in the sour cream.
5. Fill each crepe with the veal mixture and fold over. Place in a buttered shallow baking dish.
6. Bake in a 350°F (180°C) oven for 20 minutes. Serves 6.

# Cabbage and Beef Crepes

18 crepes
Filling:
3 tablespoons (45 g) butter
3 onions, chopped
1 clove garlic, minced
2 lb (1 kg) ground beef
2 cups chopped cabbage
½ teaspoon marjoram
¼ teaspoon chilli powder
2 teaspoons salt

½ teaspoon black pepper
⅓ cup plain flour
1½ cups chopped tomatoes
Sauce:
1 cup chopped cabbage
2 cups chopped tomatoes
1½ cups (375 ml) tomato juice
1½ tablespoons vinegar
1½ tablespoons sugar
salt and pepper

1. Make the crepes using the Basic Crepe Batter recipe (see Index). Set aside.
2. Sauté the onions and garlic in the butter until the onions are golden brown.
3. Add the beef, cabbage, marjoram, chilli powder, salt, pepper, flour and 1½ cups chopped tomatoes. Blend thoroughly and cook, covered, for ½ hour.
4. Fill each crepe with the beef mixture and fold over. Place in a buttered shallow baking dish and bake in a 350°F (180°C) oven for 20 minutes.
5. Combine all the ingredients for the sauce in a saucepan and simmer for 15 minutes. Season to taste with salt and pepper.
6. Put the heated crepes on a serving and pour on the sauce. Serve immediately. Serves 6.

# Bolognese Crepes

18 crepes
2½ tablespoons olive oil
2 cloves garlic, minced
2 medium onions, chopped
2½ tablespoons chopped parsley
2 lb (1 kg) ground beef

2½ tablespoons plain flour
1 lb (500 g) canned tomatoes,
  drained and chopped
2 cups grated Mozzarella cheese
grated Parmesan cheese

1. Make the crepes using the Basic Crepe Batter recipe (see Index). Set aside.
2. Sauté the garlic and onions in the olive oil until the onions are golden brown.
3. Add the parsley and ground beef and cook until the meat is brown. Stir frequently to break up the meat.
4. Sprinkle on the flour and mix well.
5. Add the canned tomatoes and Mozzarella cheese. Blend thoroughly.
6. Fill each crepe with the meat mixture and fold up. Place in a buttered shallow baking dish.
7. Bake in a 350°F (180°C) oven for 20 minutes.
8. Sprinkle with Parmesan cheese and serve immediately. Serves 6.

# Roman Crepes

18 crepes
2 tablespoons olive oil
2 lb (1 kg) Italian sausage
½ lb (250 g) mushrooms
⅔ cup chopped green pepper
2 cloves garlic, minced
⅔ cup chopped onion

2½ tablespoons chopped parsley
½ teaspoon crushed bay leaves
salt and pepper
1½ cups chopped Mozzarella
  cheese
1½ cups ricotta cheese
18 anchovy fillets

1. Make the crepes using the Basic Crepe Batter recipe (see Index). Set aside.
2. Chop the sausage and the mushrooms into small cubes and sauté in the oil with the green pepper, garlic, onion, parsley and bay leaves.
3. Season to taste with salt and pepper.
4. Fill each crepe with the sausage mixture.
5. Before folding up, sprinkle with the Mozzarella and ricotta cheeses and top with an anchovy fillet.
6. Fold over and place in a buttered shallow baking dish.
7. Bake in a 350°F (180°C) oven for 15 minutes. Serves 6.

# Italian Sausage Crepes

18 crepes
1 lb (500 g) Italian sausage
3 cups cooked beef, chopped
3 cups cooked chopped spinach
½ cup grated Parmesan cheese
1½ teaspoons salt
½ teaspoon black pepper

White Sauce:
⅓ cup (85 g) butter
⅓ cup plain flour
3 cups (750 ml) milk
1 teaspoon salt
¼ teaspoon black pepper
chopped chives

1.  Make the crepes using the Basic Crepe Batter or Spinach Crepe Batter recipe (see Index). Set aside.
2.  Chop the Italian sausage into small bits.
3.  Mix the sausage with the beef, spinach, Parmesan cheese, salt and pepper. Set aside.
4.  Make the white sauce by melting the butter in a saucepan. Remove from the heat and stir in the flour. Return to a low heat and cook for three minutes.
5.  Slowly add the milk, stirring constantly, and cook until thickened.
6.  Add the salt and pepper and blend thoroughly.
7.  Fill each crepe with the sausage mixture. Fold over and place in a buttered shallow baking dish.
8.  Pour on the white sauce and bake in a 350°F (180°C) oven for 20-30 minutes.
9.  Serve sprinkled with chopped chives.

Serves 6.

# Steak and Kidney Crepes

18 crepes
½ cup (125 g) butter
3 medium onions, chopped
2 cloves garlic, minced
½ lb (250 g) lamb kidneys
1½ lb (750 g) chuck steak

1 cup (250 ml) red wine
4 tablespoons plain flour
3 cups (750 ml) beef stock
2 teaspoons salt
½ teaspoon black pepper
chopped parsley

1. Make the crepes using the Basic Crepe Batter recipe (see Index). Set aside.
2. Sauté the onions and garlic in the butter in a large saucepan until the onions are golden brown.
3. Dice the kidneys and chuck steak and add to the onions. Cook over a medium heat, stirring constantly, until the meat is well-browned.
4. Stir in the red wine and bring to a boil. Remove from heat.
5. Sprinkle on the flour and blend thoroughly. Return to the heat.
6. Pour on the beef stock, stirring constantly.
7. Add the salt and pepper. Cover and cook over a low heat until the meat is tender.
8. Fill the crepes with the meat mixture and fold over. Place in a buttered shallow baking dish.
9. Bake in a 350°F (180°C) oven for 15 minutes.
10. Serve sprinkled with chopped parsley.

Serves 6.

# Creamy Chicken Crepes

18 crepes
½ cup (125 g) butter
½ cup plain flour
¼ cup chopped parsley
2½ tablespoons chopped chives

½ teaspoon dried tarragon
1 teaspoon salt
½ teaspoon black pepper
3 cups (750 ml) cream
4 cups diced cooked chicken

1. Make the crepes using the Basic Crepe Batter or Herb Crepe Batter recipe (see Index). Set aside.
2. Melt the butter in a large saucepan. Remove from the heat and stir in the flour until smooth. Return to a low heat and cook for three minutes.
3. Stir in the parsley, chives, tarragon, salt and pepper.
4. Slowly add the cream, stirring constantly. Cook until thickened.
5. Add the chicken and heat through.
6. Fill each crepe with the chicken mixture using a slotted spoon to remove the chicken. Fold over and place in a buttered shallow baking dish.
7. Pour over the remaining sauce and bake in a 350°F (180°C) oven for 15 minutes. Serves 6.

# Chinese-Beef Crepes

18 crepes
2 lb (1 kg) ground beef
2 eggs, beaten
2 teaspoons salt
2 teaspoons Worcestershire sauce

⅔ cup grated Swiss cheese
1 cup grated Cheddar cheese
¼ cup crumbled blue vein cheese
¼ lb (125 g) cream cheese
4 tablespoons sour cream

1. Make the crepes using the Basic Crepe Batter or Cheesey Crepe Batter recipe (see Index). Set aside.
2. Thoroughly blend the beef with the eggs, salt and Worcestershire sauce.
3. Cook over a medium heat, stirring frequently, until the meat is well-browned. Remove any fat from the cooked meat.
4. Stir in the cheeses and sour cream.
5. Fill each crepe with the mixture and fold over. Place in a buttered shallow baking dish.
6. Bake in a 350°F (180°C) oven for 15 minutes. Serves 6.

# Beef Stroganoff Crepes

| | |
|---|---|
| 18 crepes | 2 teaspoons Worcestershire sauce |
| ⅓ cup (85 g) butter | ⅓ cup (85 ml) tomato sauce |
| 1 onion, chopped | ⅓ cup (85 ml) red wine |
| 2 cloves garlic, minced | ½ teaspoon black pepper |
| ½ lb (250 g) fresh mushrooms | ⅓ cup (85 ml) beef stock |
| 2 lb (1 kg) rump steak | 2 teaspoons salt |
| ¼ teaspoon ground cumin | 2 cups (500 g) sour cream |
| ¼ teaspoon marjoram | chopped chives |

1. Make the crepes using the Basic Crepe Batter recipe (see Index). Set aside and keep warm.
2. Sauté the onion and garlic in the butter until the onion is transparent.
3. Wipe the mushrooms with a damp cloth and slice thinly. Add the mushrooms to the onion and garlic and cook for five minutes.
4. Cut the steak into thin strips and add to the mushroom mixture with the cumin, marjoram, Worcestershire sauce and tomato sauce. Cook, stirring frequently, until the meat is browned.
5. Add the wine, stock, salt and pepper and cook until the meat is tender.
6. Add the sour cream, blend thoroughly and cook over a low heat until the mixture is warm.
7. Fill each crepe with the stroganoff mixture. Fold over and place in a buttered shallow baking dish.
8. Bake in a 350°F (180°C) oven for about 20 minutes or until heated through.
9. Sprinkle with chopped chives and serve. Serves 6.

# Ham Crepes

18 crepes
⅓ cup (85 g) butter
⅓ cup plain flour
4 cups (1 liter) milk
1 teaspoon salt
½ teaspoon black pepper
2 tablespoons prepared French mustard

2 lb (1 kg) cooked ham, cubed
1 lb (500 g) Cheddar cheese, cubed
2 cups green peas, cooked
1½ cups grated Swiss cheese
chopped chives

1. Make the crepes using the Basic Crepe Batter or Cheesey Crepe Batter recipe (see Index). Set aside.
2. Melt the butter in a large saucepan. Remove from heat and stir in the flour until smooth. Return to a low heat and cook for three minutes.
3. Slowly add the milk to the saucepan, stirring constantly. Cook until thickened. Remove one cup of the sauce from the pan and set aside.
4. Stir in the salt, pepper, mustard, ham, cheese and peas. Blend thoroughly and heat through.
5. Fill each crepe with the ham mixture. Fold over and place in a buttered shallow baking dish.
6. Pour the cup of reserved sauce over the crepes and sprinkle on the grated Swiss cheese.
7. Bake in a 350°F (180°C) oven for about 20 minutes.
8. Serve sprinkled with chopped chives.

Serves 6.

# Chicken Crepes with Tangerine Sauce

| | |
|---|---|
| 18 crepes | **Tangarine Sauce:** |
| ½ cup (125 g) butter | 1½ cups (375 ml) tangerine syrup |
| 1 cup chopped scallions | 2 tablespoons soy sauce |
| 1 cup chopped celery | 1 teaspoon grated fresh ginger |
| ¼ cup chopped parsley | ¼ teaspoon black pepper |
| 4 cups diced cooked chicken | 1¼ tablespoons cornstarch |
| 1½ lb (750 g) canned tangerines | 4 tablespoons cold water |

1. Make the crepes using the Basic Crepe Batter or Orange Crepe Batter (omitting sugar) recipe (see Index). Set aside.
2. Melt the butter in a large saucepan and sauté the scallions, celery and parsley for two minutes.
3. Add the chicken and mix well. Cook until the chicken is heated through.
4. Drain the tangerines and stir half into the chicken mixture. Set aside.
5. Mix the tangerine syrup, soy sauce, ginger and pepper in a saucepan. Heat until warm.
6. Mix the cornstarch with the cold water and then stir into the tangerine syrup mixture. Cook until thickened and clear.
7. Pour about ⅔ cup of the sauce into the chicken mixture.
8. Stir the remaining tangerines into the sauce and heat through.
9. Fill each crepe with some of the chicken mixture. Fold over and place in a buttered shallow baking dish.
10. Pour the sauce over the crepes and bake in a 350°F (180°C) oven for about 20 minutes.

Serves 6.

# Chicken Liver and Grape Crepes

| | |
|---|---|
| 18 crepes | 2 teaspoons Worcestershire |
| 2 lb (1 kg) chicken livers | sauce |
| ½ cup (125 g) butter | ½ lb (250 g) green grapes, halved |
| 1 medium onion, chopped | ¼ cup (65 ml) dry sherry |
| ¼ cup chopped parsley | ½ cup (125 ml) beef stock |
| ½ teaspoon grated fresh ginger | ⅔ cup (165 g) sour cream |
| 1 teaspoon salt | ⅔ cup grated mild cheese |
| ¼ teaspoon black pepper | ¼ cup chopped chives |

1. Make the crepes using the Basic Crepe Batter or Bran Crepe Batter recipe (see Index). Set aside.
2. Sauté the chicken livers in the butter, stirring constantly, over a medium heat for five minutes.
3. Add the onion and, stirring frequently, cook for another five minutes.
4. Add the parsley, ginger, salt, pepper, Worcestershire sauce, grapes, sherry and beef stock. Blend thoroughly, cover and cook for three to five minutes or until the livers are just cooked. Do not overcook the livers or they become dry.
5. Remove from heat and stir in the sour cream.
6. Fill each crepe with some of the chicken liver filling. Fold over and place in a buttered shallow baking dish.
7. Sprinkle on the grated cheese and bake in a 350°F (180°C) oven for about ten minutes.
8. Serve immediately garnished with chopped chives.

Serves 6.

# Shrimp Crepes with Nutty Cheese Sauce

18 crepes
2 lb (1 kg) ricotta cheese
4 eggs, beaten
2 cloves garlic, minced
⅔ cup grated Parmesan cheese
1 teaspoon oregano
1 teaspoon salt

2 teaspoons basil
⅔ cup chopped walnuts
¼ cup chopped parsley
2¼ tablespoons vegetable oil
3 cups chopped cooked shrimps
4 tablespoons melted butter
1 cup (250 ml) cream

1. Make the crepes using the Basic Crepe Batter recipe (see Index). Set aside.
2. Cream the ricotta cheese, then beat in the eggs.
3. Add the garlic, Parmesan cheese, oregano, salt, basil, walnuts, parsley and vegetable oil.
4. Stir two-thirds of the mixture into the chopped shrimps.
5. Fill each crepe with the mixture. Fold over and place in a buttered shallow baking dish.
6. Bake in a 350°F (180°C) oven for ½ hour.
7. In an electric blender, whirl the remaining sauce with the melted butter and cream. Pour into a saucepan and gently heat. Do not boil.
8. Pour over the crepes and serve immediately.

Serves 6.

# New Orleans Shrimp Crepes

18 crepes
1½ lb (750 g) cooked chopped
   shrimps
1 cup chopped tomatoes
1½ lb tablespoons chopped chives
2 hard-boiled eggs, chopped

½ cup chopped celery
⅓ cup chopped black olives
salt and pepper
1 cup (250 g) sour cream
⅓ cup chilli sauce
chopped parsley

1. Make the crepes using the Basic Crepe Batter recipe (see Index). Set aside.
2. Mix together the shrimps, tomatoes, chives, eggs, celery, olives and salt and pepper to taste.
3. Fill the crepes with the mixture and fold over.
4. Blend the sour cream with the chilli sauce and pour over the crepes.
5. Garnish with chopped parsley and serve cold.

Serves 6.

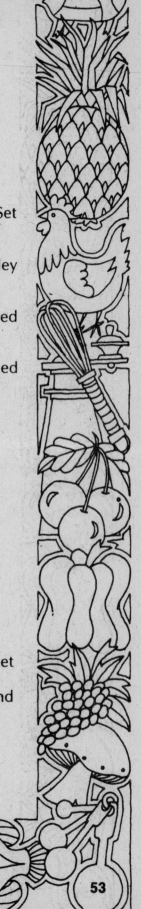

# Lobster Newburg Crepes

18 crepes
½ cup (125 g) butter
½ cup plain flour
1½ cups (375 ml) milk
1½ cups (375 ml) cream
½ cup (125 ml) dry sherry

¼ teaspoon paprika
¼ teaspoon nutmeg
¼ teaspoon cayenne pepper
2 eggs, separated
4 cups cooked, diced lobster
   meat

1. Make the crepes using the Basic Crepe Batter or Beer Crepe Batter recipe (see Index). Set aside.
2. Melt the butter in the top of a double boiler. Stir in the flour until smooth and cook for five minutes over simmering water.
3. Slowly add the milk and cream, stirring constantly. Cook until thick and smooth.
4. Add the sherry, paprika, nutmeg and cayenne pepper.
5. Add the egg yolks one at a time, beating well after each addition. Cook until thickened.
6. Mix two-thirds of the sauce with the lobster meat.
7. Fill each crepe with the lobster mixture. Fold over and place in a buttered shallow baking dish.
8. Brush the crepes with the egg whites and bake in a 350°F (180°C) oven for about 15 minutes.
9. Serve the crepes with the remaining sauce.

Serves 6.

# Scallop and Mushroom Crepes

18 crepes
2 lb (1 kg) fresh scallops
½ cup (125 ml) lemon juice
1 cup (250 ml) white wine
⅔ cup (165 ml) water
½ teaspoon salt
¼ teaspoon black pepper
½ lb (250 g) fresh mushrooms
¾ cup (185 g) butter

½ cup plain flour
2 cups (500 ml) milk
1 teaspoon salt
¼ teaspoon black pepper
½ teaspoon dry mustard
⅛ teaspoon cayenne pepper
½ lb (250 g) grated cheese
paprika
chopped chives

1. Make the crepes using the Basic Crepe Batter recipe (see Index). Set aside.
2. Mix together the scallops, lemon juice, wine, water, salt and pepper in a large saucepan. Bring to a boil. Reduce heat, cover and cook until the scallops are tender. Drain.
3. Wipe the mushrooms with a damp cloth. If small, cut in half. If large, slice. Sauté the mushrooms in ¼ cup (65 g) of the butter for five minutes. Set aside.
4. Melt the remaining ½ cup of butter in a saucepan. Remove from heat and stir in the flour until smooth. Return to a low heat and cook for three minutes.
5. Slowly stir in the milk and cook, stirring constantly, until thick and smooth.
6. Add the salt, pepper, mustard, cayenne pepper and grated cheese. Cook over a low heat until the cheese melts.
7. Pour two-thirds of the sauce into the scallop mixture.
8. Add the mushrooms and mix well.
9. Fill each crepe with some of the filling. Fold over and place in a buttered shallow baking dish.
10. Pour the remaining sauce over the crepes and bake in a 350°F (180°C) oven for about 20 minutes.
11. Serve sprinkled with paprika and chopped chives.

Serves 6.

# Tahitian Chicken Crepes

18 crepes
2 lb (1 kg) boned chicken
2½ tablespoons soy sauce
2½ tablespoons olive oil
1¼ tablespoons brown sugar
2½ tablespoons vinegar
1 teaspoon grated fresh ginger
1 teaspoon grated lemon rind
½ cup (125 ml) vegetable oil

3 medium bananas, diced
1 lb (500 g) canned crushed
  pineapple

Sauce:
2½ tablespoons honey
2½ tablespoons soy sauce
2½ tablespoons cornstarch
1 cup (250 ml) pineapple liquid

1. Make the crepes using the Basic Crepe Batter or the Herb Crepe Batter recipe. (see Index). Set aside.
2. Cut the chicken in small cubes.
3. Mix together the soy sauce, olive oil, brown sugar, vinegar, ginger and lemon rind.
4. Pour this soy sauce mixture over the chicken and mix well to ensure that the chicken is well-coated with the mixture. Set aside to marinate for about 30 — 45 minutes.
5. Heat the vegetable oil in a large frypan and sauté the chicken for 15 minutes or until tender.
6. Stir in the bananas and cook for another two minutes.
7. Drain the pineapple (reserve the liquid) and add to the chicken and banana mixture. Cover and cook for another three minutes.
8. Fill each crepe with some of the filling and place on a buttered shallow baking dish.
9. Bake in a 350°F (180°C) oven for about 15 minutes.
10. In a small saucepan mix together the honey, soy sauce, cornstarch (mixed with a little pineapple liquid) and the pineapple liquid. Cook over a low heat, stirring constantly, until the sauce thickens and clears.
11. Pour the sauce over the crepes and serve immediately.

Serves 6.

# Sweet Crepes

## Walnut-Coconut Crepes

6 crepes
¼ cup (65 g) butter
¼ cup sugar
1 cup chopped walnuts

2 cups shredded coconut
vanilla ice cream
glace cherries

1. Make the crepes using the Sweet Crepe Batter or French Crepe Batter recipe (see Index). Place on a baking sheet.
2. Cream together the butter and sugar. Spread on the crepes. Leave the crepes flat; do not fold over.
3. Combine the walnuts and the coconut. Sprinkle half the mixture on the crepes.
4. Place crepes under a hot broiler and cook until golden brown. Cool before removing from sheet.
5. Just before serving, spread ice cream on the crepes.
6. Sprinkle with the remaining walnut-coconut mixture and top with a glace cherry.

Serves 6.

# Banana-Nut Crepes

| | |
|---|---|
| 12 crepes | ½ teaspoon cinnamon |
| 6 large bananas | ¼ cup (125 g) butter |
| 1 cup chopped nuts | ⅓ cup sugar |
| ¼ cup brown sugar | ⅓ cup (85 ml) brandy |

1. Make the crepes using the Sweet Crepe Batter recipe (see Index). Set aside.
2. Bake the bananas in their skins in a 350°F (180°C) oven for 20 minutes. Peel and cut in half lengthwise.
3. Mix together the nuts, brown sugar and cinnamon.
4. Spread the nut mixture over each crepe and place a half banana in the center. Roll up.
5. Blend together the butter and sugar in a frypan.
6. Add the brandy and cook over a low heat until the sugar has dissolved and the mixture is syrupy.
7. Put the banana-nut crepes in the frypan and cook until heated through spooning the syrup over the crepes.

Serves 6.

# Coconut Crepes

| | |
|---|---|
| 12 crepes | 1 teaspoon grated orange rind |
| ⅓ cup (85 g) butter | 1¼ cups (300 ml) cream |
| ⅔ cup brown sugar | 1½ teaspoons sugar |
| 2½ cups coconut | 1 teaspoon grated orange rind |
| ¼ cup (65 ml) orange juice | |

1. Make the crepes using the Orange Crepe Batter recipe (see Index). Set aside.
2. Melt the butter in a saucepan and add the sugar, coconut, orange juice and one teaspoon of grated orange rind. Cook over a low heat until thickened, stirring constantly.
3. Fill the crepes with the coconut mixture. Roll up and place on a buttered shallow baking dish.
4. Bake in a 350°F (180°C) oven for 7 minutes.
5. Whip the cream with the sugar and orange rind.
6. Spoon the cream over the crepes and serve immediately.

Serves 6.

# Apple Custard Crepes

8 crepes
3 green cooking apples
½ cup (125 ml) water
2 tablespoons (30 g) butter
2 teaspoons maple syrup
1½ tablespoons brown sugar

⅔ cup chopped walnuts
4 egg whites
¼ teaspoon baking powder
pinch of salt
¾ cup sugar

1. Make the crepes using the Sweet Crepe Batter or French Crepe Batter recipe (see Index). Set aside.
2. Peel and core the apples and cut into slices. Simmer in the water until just tender. Set aside.
3. Melt the butter and stir in the maple syrup and brown sugar.
4. Add to the apples with the nuts. Mix well and cook over a low heat for five minutes.
5. Beat the egg whites until fluffy. Add the baking powder and salt and beat until almost stiff. Gradually add the sugar and beat until stiff.
6. Fold the egg whites into the apple mixture.
7. Fit each crepe into an oven-proof cup or a ramekin.
8. Spoon the mixture into each crepe and bake in a 325°F (160°C) oven for 35 minutes. Remove from the oven and cool before removing from the cups or ramekins.

Serves 8.

# Lemon-Cream Cheese Crepes

8 crepes
½ lb (250 g) cream cheese
2 cups (500 ml) sweetened
  condensed milk
½ cup (125 ml) lemon juice

1 teaspoon grated lemon rind
¾ teaspoon vanilla essence
whipped cream
grated orange rind

1. Make the crepes using the Basic Crepe Batter or Lemon Crepe Batter recipe (see Index). Set aside.
2. Mix together the cream cheese, condensed milk, lemon juice, grated lemon rind and vanilla essence. Beat until smooth. Put in the refrigerator for two hours.
3. Spread the mixture on each of the crepes and roll up.
4. Spoon on the whipped cream and sprinkle with grated orange rind.

Serves 4.

# Grape and Yogurt Crepes

**8 crepes**
**2 cups (500 g) plain yogurt**
**½ teaspoon grated fresh ginger**
**2 cups green grape halves**
**mandarin sections**

1. Make the crepes using the Sweet Crepe Batter recipe (see Index). Set aside.
2. Combine 1½ cups of yogurt with the ginger and grapes.
3. Fill each crepe with the mixture and fold over.
4. Dot each crepe with the remaining yogurt and decorate with mandarin sections.

Serves 4.

# Chocolate Nut Crepes

**12 crepes**
**⅓ cup cocoa**
**⅔ cup cornstarch**
**½ cup sugar**

**4 cups (1 liter) milk**
**1 cup chopped walnuts**
**whipped cream**
**shaved dark chocolate**

1. Make the crepes using the Sweet Crepe Batter or Chocolate Crepe Batter recipe (see Index). Set aside and keep warm.
2. Mix the cocoa, cornstarch and sugar together in a saucepan.
3. Add a little milk and blend thoroughly.
4. Gradually add the rest of the milk, mixing constantly.
5. Place over a medium heat and cook, stirring continually, until the mixture is thick.
6. Add the nuts and mix well.
7. Fill the crepes with the chocolate nut mixture and roll up.
8. Place on dessert dishes and serve immediately with whipped cream sprinkled with shaved chocolate.

Serves 6.

# Raisin and Cream Cheese Crepes

12 crepes
1 cup raisins
⅓ cup (85 ml) boiling water
¾ lb (375 g) cream cheese

½ cup sugar
½ teaspoon cinnamon
grated lemon rind
confectioner's sugar

1. Make the crepes using the Sweet Crepe Batter or French Crepe Batter recipe (see Index). Set aside and keep warm.
2. Soak the raisins in the boiling water for 15 minutes. Drain.
3. Soften the cream cheese, then beat with the sugar and cinnamon until smooth.
4. Add the raisins and blend thoroughly.
5. Fill each crepe with the mixture and roll up.
6. Sprinkle with grated lemon rind and confectioner's sugar. Serve immediately.

Serves 6.

# Mixed Fruit Crepes

12 crepes
3 cups mixed dried fruit
1 cup (250 ml) boiling water
½ cup orange marmalade
whipped cream

1. Make the crepes using the Sweet Crepe Batter or Orange Crepe Batter recipe (see Index). Set aside and keep warm.
2. Pour the boiling water over the mixed dried fruit and allow to soak for 15 minutes, stirring frequently. Drain.
3. Add the orange marmalade and blend thoroughly.
4. Fill each crepe with some of the mixture and fold over.
5. Serve immediately with whipped cream.

Serves 6.

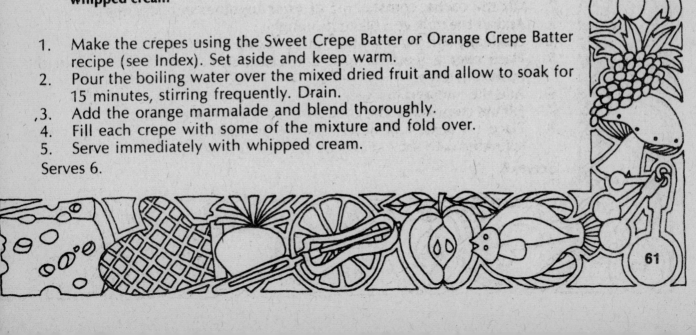

# Strawberry-Sour Cream Crepes

12 crepes
2 cups (500 g) sour cream
⅓ cup sugar
2 cups sliced strawberries
confectioner's sugar

1. Make the crepes using the Sweet Crepe Batter or French Crepe Batter recipe (see Index). Set aside.
2. Beat together the sour cream and sugar.
3. Fold in the strawberries.
4. Fill each crepe with the mixture and fold over.
5. Sprinkle with confectioner's sugar and serve.

Serves 6.

# Spicy Apple Crepes

12 crepes
⅓ cup (85 g) butter
8 large cooking apples
2½ tablespoons lemon juice

1 teaspoon grated lemon rind
½ teaspoon cinnamon
¼ teaspoon mixed spice
⅔ cup sugar

1. Make the crepes using the Sweet Crepe Batter recipe (see Index). Set aside.
2. Peel and core the apples. Cut into ½-inch (1-cm) slices.
3. Melt the butter in a saucepan and gently cook the apples with the lemon juice, lemon rind, cinnamon and mixed spice over a low heat for five minutes.
4. Add the sugar and cook until the apples are just tender. Cool slightly.
5. Fill the crepes with the apple mixture. Fold over and place in a buttered shallow baking dish.
6. Bake in a 350°F (180°C) oven for 15 minutes.

Serves 6.

# Applesauce Crepes

12 crepes
4 cups puréed apples
½ cup sugar
1 teaspoon cinnamon
2 tablespoons cornstarch
3 tablespoons cold water

⅔ cup (165 g) butter
4 tablespoons sugar
confectioner's sugar
cinnamon
nutmeg

1. Make the crepes using the Sweet Crepe Batter recipe (see Index). Set aside.
2. Mix the puréed apples with the sugar and cinnamon in a saucepan.
3. Blend together the cornstarch and cold water and add to the apples. Cook over a medium heat until thickened.
4. Fill the crepes with the applesauce and fold over.
5. Melt the butter in a large frypan and put in the crepes.
6. Sprinkle with the four tablespoons of sugar, cover and cook until golden brown.
7. Serve sprinkled with confectioner's sugar, cinnamon and nutmeg.

Serves 6.

# Russian Crepes

12 crepes
½ cup sugar
3 eggs, separated
pinch cardamom
⅛ teaspoon salt
1 cup (250 g) cottage cheese

½ cup chopped glace cherries
⅓ cup sultana raisins
⅓ cup glace orange peel
2 tablespoons glace lemon peel
3 egg whites

1. Make the crepes using the Sweet Crepe Batter recipe (see Index). Set aside and keep warm.
2. Beat the sugar with the egg yolks until thick.
3. Add the cardamom, salt, cottage cheese, cherries, sultana raisins, orange and lemon peel. Mix thoroughly.
4. Beat the six egg whites until stiff and fold into the cottage cheese mixture.
5. Fill each crepe with the mixture and fold over.
6. Place in a buttered shallow baking dish and put under a hot broiler for three to four minutes. Serve immediately.

Serves 6.

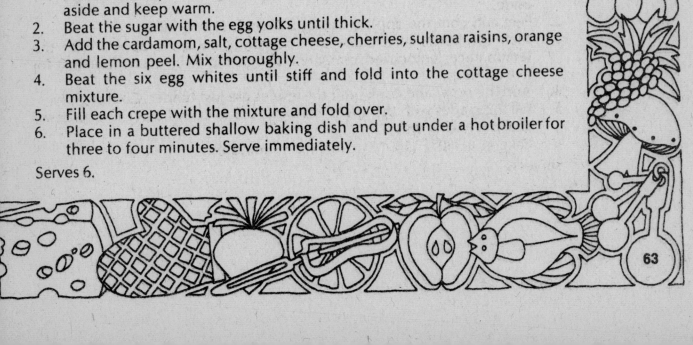

# Chocolate Mousse Crepes

12 crepes
½ lb (250 g) semisweet chocolate
2 teaspoons sugar
1½ teaspoons vanilla essence

½ cup (125 ml) boiling water
5 eggs, separated
whipped cream
chopped nuts

1. Make the crepes using the Sweet Crepe Batter or Chocolate Crepe Batter recipe (see Index). Set aside.
2. Grate the chocolate (or grind in an electric blender).
3. Mix the chocolate with the sugar, vanilla essence and boiling water. Beat until smooth.
4. Add the egg yolks one at a time beating well after each addition.
5. Beat the egg whites until stiff. Fold gently into the chocolate mixture. Refrigerate for two hours.
6. Fill each crepe with the chocolate mousse mixture and fold over.
7. Serve with whipped cream and sprinkle with chopped nuts.

Serves 6.

# Honolulu Crepes

18 crepes
⅓ cup (85 g) butter
3 small onions, sliced
1 green pepper, sliced
1 red pepper, sliced
1 lb (500 g) canned pineapple chunks (with liquid)

2½ tablespoons honey
2½ tablespoons vinegar
2½ tablespoons soy sauce
5 tablespoons cornstarch
2 cups (500 ml) chicken stock
6 cups cooked diced chicken
½ cup chopped Macadamian nuts

1. Make the crepes using the Basic Crepe Batter recipe (see Index). Set aside and keep warm.
2. Sauté the onions and peppers in the butter until tender.
3. Add the pineapple and honey and mix well.
4. Blend the cornstarch with the vinegar, soy sauce and a little of the chicken stock. Add to the pineapple mixture and mix thoroughly.
5. Add the remaining chicken stock, stirring constantly. Cook until thickened.
6. Add the diced chicken and chopped nuts. Heat through.
7. Fill each crepe with the mixture and serve immediately.

Serves 6.

# Hot Fudge Crepes

12 crepes
½ cup (125 g) butter
1 cup sugar
¾ teaspoon instant coffee
   powder

⅓ cup cocoa
1 cup (250 ml) cream
1¼ teaspoons vanilla essence
chocolate ice cream
chopped nuts

1. Make the crepes using the Sweet Crepe Batter or Chocolate Crepe Batter recipe (see Index). Set aside.
2. Melt the butter in a saucepan and add the sugar, instant coffee and cocoa. Blend thoroughly.
3. Gradually add the cream and cook over a medium heat, stirring constantly, for about five minutes.
4. Remove from the heat and add the vanilla essence.
5. Put small scoops of chocolate ice cream on each crepe and fold over.
6. Pour the hot fudge sauce over the crepes and sprinkle with chopped nuts. Serve immediately.

Serves 6.

# Choc-Coconut Crepes

12 crepes
¾ lb (375 g) milk chocolate
⅔ cup (165 ml) water
2 tablespoons (30 g) butter
⅔ cup (165 ml) cream
1½ cups desiccated coconut

1. Make the crepes using the French Crepe Batter recipe (see Index). Set aside and keep warm.
2. Melt the chocolate with the water and butter in a saucepan.
3. Gradually add the cream, stirring constantly.
4. Add the coconut and blend thoroughly.
5. Fill each crepe with the mixture and fold over. Serve immediately.

Serves 6.

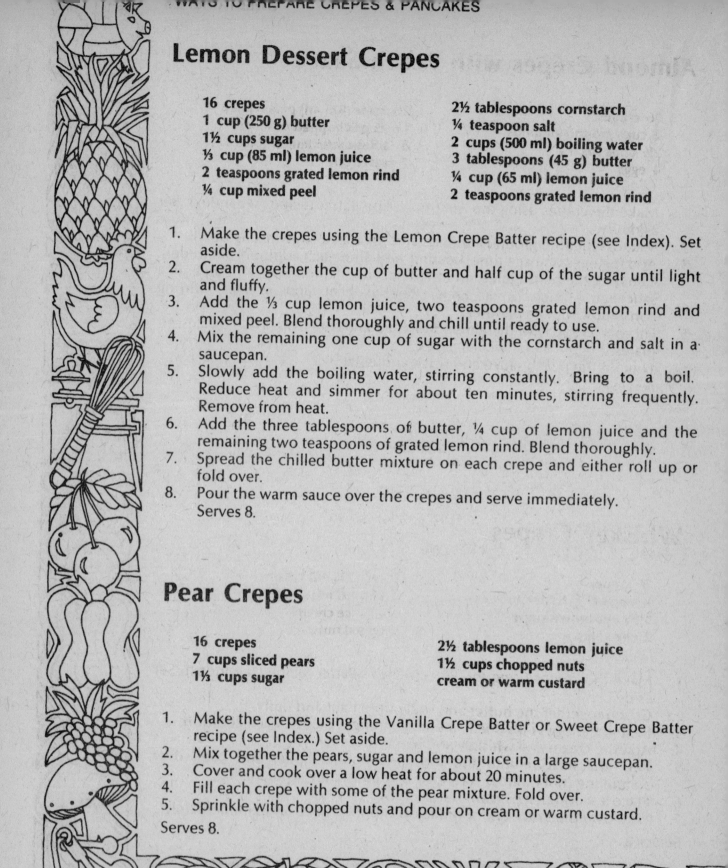

# Lemon Dessert Crepes

| | |
|---|---|
| 16 crepes | 2½ tablespoons cornstarch |
| 1 cup (250 g) butter | ¼ teaspoon salt |
| 1½ cups sugar | 2 cups (500 ml) boiling water |
| ⅓ cup (85 ml) lemon juice | 3 tablespoons (45 g) butter |
| 2 teaspoons grated lemon rind | ¼ cup (65 ml) lemon juice |
| ¼ cup mixed peel | 2 teaspoons grated lemon rind |

1. Make the crepes using the Lemon Crepe Batter recipe (see Index). Set aside.
2. Cream together the cup of butter and half cup of the sugar until light and fluffy.
3. Add the ⅓ cup lemon juice, two teaspoons grated lemon rind and mixed peel. Blend thoroughly and chill until ready to use.
4. Mix the remaining one cup of sugar with the cornstarch and salt in a saucepan.
5. Slowly add the boiling water, stirring constantly. Bring to a boil. Reduce heat and simmer for about ten minutes, stirring frequently. Remove from heat.
6. Add the three tablespoons of butter, ¼ cup of lemon juice and the remaining two teaspoons of grated lemon rind. Blend thoroughly.
7. Spread the chilled butter mixture on each crepe and either roll up or fold over.
8. Pour the warm sauce over the crepes and serve immediately.
   Serves 8.

# Pear Crepes

| | |
|---|---|
| 16 crepes | 2½ tablespoons lemon juice |
| 7 cups sliced pears | 1½ cups chopped nuts |
| 1⅓ cups sugar | cream or warm custard |

1. Make the crepes using the Vanilla Crepe Batter or Sweet Crepe Batter recipe (see Index.) Set aside.
2. Mix together the pears, sugar and lemon juice in a large saucepan.
3. Cover and cook over a low heat for about 20 minutes.
4. Fill each crepe with some of the pear mixture. Fold over.
5. Sprinkle with chopped nuts and pour on cream or warm custard.

Serves 8.

# Almond Crepes with Peach Sauce

16 crepes
2 cups ground almonds
2½ cups sugar
4 eggs

2½ cups (625 ml) peach juice
1½ cups chopped peaches
3 tablespoons lemon juice
1 cup sugar

1. Make the crepes using the Almond Crepe Batter recipe (see Index). Set aside.
2. Mix together the ground almonds and sugar in a large mixing bowl.
3. Add the eggs one at a time, beating well after each addition. Set aside.
4. Combine the peach juice, chopped peaches, lemon juice and sugar in a saucepan. Bring to a boil. Reduce heat and simmer, stirring constantly, for five minutes.
5. Fill each crepe with the almond mixture and fold over. Place on dessert plates.
6. Pour on the peach sauce and serve immediately.
   Serves 8.

# Whiskey Crepes

16 crepes
⅓ cup (85 g) butter
1⅔ cups brown sugar
2 egg yolks

1 cup (250 ml) cream
¼ cup (65 ml) whiskey
vanilla ice cream
chopped nuts

1. Make the crepes using the French Crepe Batter recipe (see Index). Set aside.
2. Cream together the butter and sugar until light and fluffy.
3. Beat in the egg yolks one at a time, beating well after each addition.
4. Add the cream and whiskey and blend thoroughly.
5. Pour the mixture into the top of a double boiler and cook over simmering (not boiling) water, stirring constantly, until thick.
6. Place a scoop of ice cream between two crepes.
7. Pour over the sauce and sprinkle on chopped nuts. Serve immediately.

Serves 8.

# Nutty Apple Crepes

16 crepes
6 large cooking apples
½ cup (125 g) butter
1 cup sugar
3 teaspoons cinnamon
1 cup chopped nuts

1. Make the crepes using the Sweet Crepe Batter recipe (see Index). Set aside and keep warm.
2. Peel, core and slice the apples.
3. Melt the butter in a large frypan.
4. Mix together the sugar and cinnamon and stir into the butter.
5. Add the apple slices and cook gently until the sugar begins to caramelize.
6. Fill each crepe with the apple mixture and fold over.
7. Sprinkle on the nuts and serve immediately. Serves 8.

# Cream Cheese Crepes with Peach Sauce

16 crepes
4 tablespoons (60 g) butter
1 cup sugar
2 cups sliced fresh peaches (or well-drained canned peaches)
2 tablespoons lemon juice
½ cup sugar
1 lb (500 g) cream cheese
¾ cup (185 g) sour cream
1 tablespoon vanilla essence
1 cup (250 g) butter
3 teaspoons grated lemon

1. Make the crepes using the French Crepe Batter or Sweet Crepe Batter recipe (see Index). Set aside.
2. Melt the butter in a large saucepan and add the sugar. Blend thoroughly.
3. Add the peaches and lemon juice and cook over a low heat for ten minutes, stirring frequently. Remove from heat.
4. Thoroughly blend the ½ cup sugar, cream cheese, sour cream, vanilla essence, butter and lemon rind. Beat well.
5. Fill each crepe with the cream cheese mixture. Fold over and place in a buttered shallow baking dish.
6. Bake in a 350°F (180°C) oven for about 15 minutes or until well heated.
7. Remove to serving dishes and pour on the warm peach sauce. Serve immediately. Serves 8.

# Crepes Suzette

18 crepes
⅔ cup (165 g) butter
5 tablespoons sugar
1½ tablespoons grated orange rind
1 teaspoon grated lemon rind

½ cup (125 ml) orange juice
1½ tablespoons lemon juice
¼ cup (65 ml) Grand Marnier
½ cup (125 ml) cognac

1. Make the crepes using the Sweet Crepe Batter recipe (see Index). Set aside.
2. Cream together the butter, sugar, orange and lemon rinds.
3. Put the butter mixture into a large frypan or chafing dish and heat until melted, stirring constantly.
4. Add the orange and lemon juice and Grand Marnier and mix well. Cook until the sauce thickens.
5. Put the crepes one by one into the sauce and when soaked, fold into quarters and move aside. Repeat until all the crepes are soaked and folded.
6. Heat the cognac slightly and pour over the crepes. Ignite and serve when the flame has gone out. Serves 6.

# Creme de Cacao Crepes

16 crepes
½ cup (125 g) butter
1¼ cups confectioner's sugar
2 eggs, separated

¼ cup (65 ml) creme de cacao
vanilla ice cream
½ cup grated dark chocolate

1. Make the crepes using the Chocolate Crepe Batter or Vanilla Crepe Batter recipe (see Index). Set aside.
2. Mix together the butter and sugar in the top of a double boiler. Place over simmering water.
3. Beat in the egg yolks one at a time, beating thoroughly after each addition. Remove from the heat and cool slightly.
4. Beat the egg whites until stiff. Add the creme de cacao and blend thoroughly.
5. Fold the egg whites into the egg yolk mixture.
6. Put a scoop of vanilla ice cream between two crepes.
7. Pour the creme de cacao sauce over and sprinkle with grated chocolate. Serves 8.

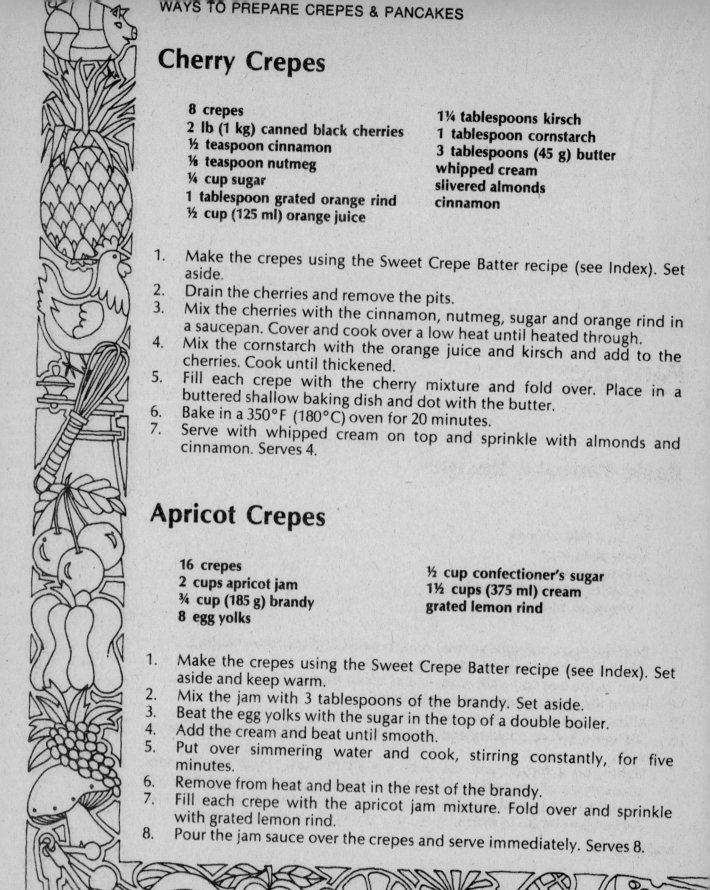

# Cherry Crepes

8 crepes
2 lb (1 kg) canned black cherries
½ teaspoon cinnamon
⅛ teaspoon nutmeg
¼ cup sugar
1 tablespoon grated orange rind
½ cup (125 ml) orange juice

1¼ tablespoons kirsch
1 tablespoon cornstarch
3 tablespoons (45 g) butter
whipped cream
slivered almonds
cinnamon

1. Make the crepes using the Sweet Crepe Batter recipe (see Index). Set aside.
2. Drain the cherries and remove the pits.
3. Mix the cherries with the cinnamon, nutmeg, sugar and orange rind in a saucepan. Cover and cook over a low heat until heated through.
4. Mix the cornstarch with the orange juice and kirsch and add to the cherries. Cook until thickened.
5. Fill each crepe with the cherry mixture and fold over. Place in a buttered shallow baking dish and dot with the butter.
6. Bake in a 350°F (180°C) oven for 20 minutes.
7. Serve with whipped cream on top and sprinkle with almonds and cinnamon. Serves 4.

# Apricot Crepes

16 crepes
2 cups apricot jam
¾ cup (185 g) brandy
8 egg yolks

½ cup confectioner's sugar
1½ cups (375 ml) cream
grated lemon rind

1. Make the crepes using the Sweet Crepe Batter recipe (see Index). Set aside and keep warm.
2. Mix the jam with 3 tablespoons of the brandy. Set aside.
3. Beat the egg yolks with the sugar in the top of a double boiler.
4. Add the cream and beat until smooth.
5. Put over simmering water and cook, stirring constantly, for five minutes.
6. Remove from heat and beat in the rest of the brandy.
7. Fill each crepe with the apricot jam mixture. Fold over and sprinkle with grated lemon rind.
8. Pour the jam sauce over the crepes and serve immediately. Serves 8.

# Pancakes

## Basic Pancake Recipe

1 egg
1¼ cups (300 ml) milk
1 cup plain flour
½ teaspoon salt
1½ tablespoons melted butter or
   vegetable oil

1. Beat the egg until light yellow. Add the milk and continue beating.
2. Sift the flour and salt into a mixing bowl.
3. Pour in the egg and milk mixture and blend thoroughly.
4. Stir in the melted butter or vegetable oil.
5. Allow to stand for at least one hour before using.
6. Stir again before cooking and if the batter is too thick add a little more milk.
7. Lightly oil a frypan and set over a medium heat. Pour one to two tablespoons of the batter into the pan. If a thinner pancake is desired, tilt the pan to spread out the pancake. Cook until the surface is dry and the bubbles begin to break. Turn over and cook on the other side.

Makes 12-15.

# Thick Pancakes

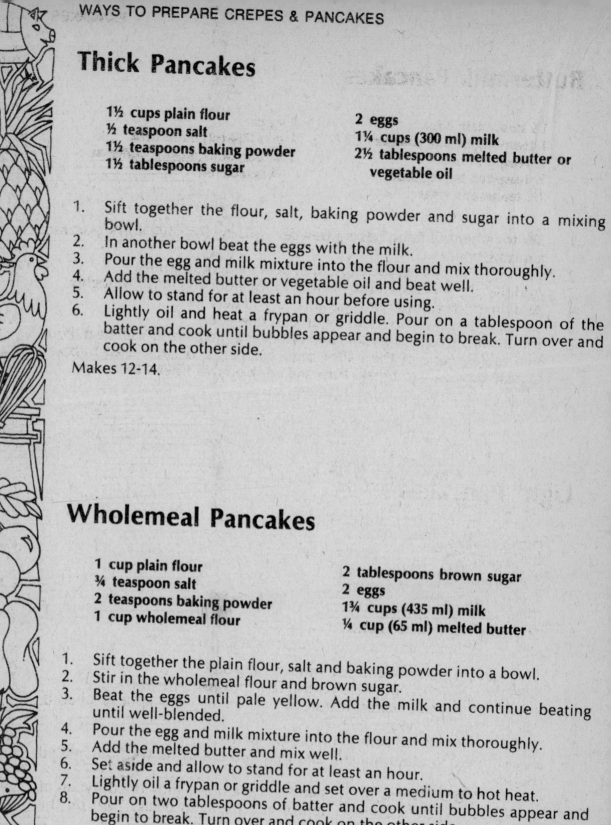

| | |
|---|---|
| 1½ cups plain flour | 2 eggs |
| ½ teaspoon salt | 1¼ cups (300 ml) milk |
| 1½ teaspoons baking powder | 2½ tablespoons melted butter or |
| 1½ tablespoons sugar | vegetable oil |

1. Sift together the flour, salt, baking powder and sugar into a mixing bowl.
2. In another bowl beat the eggs with the milk.
3. Pour the egg and milk mixture into the flour and mix thoroughly.
4. Add the melted butter or vegetable oil and beat well.
5. Allow to stand for at least an hour before using.
6. Lightly oil and heat a frypan or griddle. Pour on a tablespoon of the batter and cook until bubbles appear and begin to break. Turn over and cook on the other side.

Makes 12-14.

# Wholemeal Pancakes

| | |
|---|---|
| 1 cup plain flour | 2 tablespoons brown sugar |
| ¾ teaspoon salt | 2 eggs |
| 2 teaspoons baking powder | 1¾ cups (435 ml) milk |
| 1 cup wholemeal flour | ¼ cup (65 ml) melted butter |

1. Sift together the plain flour, salt and baking powder into a bowl.
2. Stir in the wholemeal flour and brown sugar.
3. Beat the eggs until pale yellow. Add the milk and continue beating until well-blended.
4. Pour the egg and milk mixture into the flour and mix thoroughly.
5. Add the melted butter and mix well.
6. Set aside and allow to stand for at least an hour.
7. Lightly oil a frypan or griddle and set over a medium to hot heat.
8. Pour on two tablespoons of batter and cook until bubbles appear and begin to break. Turn over and cook on the other side.

Makes 12-14.

# Buttermilk Pancakes

1½ cups plain flour
1 teaspoon baking powder
½ teaspoon salt
½ teaspoon baking soda
1½ teaspoons sugar

2 eggs
1 cup (250 ml) buttermilk
2 tablespoons melted butter or vegetable oil

1. Sift together the flour, baking powder, salt, baking soda and sugar into a mixing bowl.
2. In another bowl beat the eggs, then beat in the buttermilk.
3. Add the egg and buttermilk mixture to the flour and mix thoroughly.
4. Add the melted butter or vegetable oil and beat well.
5. Set aside and allow to stand for at least one hour.
6. Lightly oil a frypan or griddle and put over a medium to high heat. Pour two tablespoons of the batter onto the pan and cook until bubbles appear and begin to break. Turn and cook on the other side.

Makes 12-15.

# Light Pancakes

1½ cups cake flour
¼ teaspoon salt
2 eggs, separated
1 cup (250 ml) water
1 cup (250 ml) cream
1¼ tablespoons melted butter

1. Sift together the flour and salt into a mixing bowl.
2. Beat the egg yolks until pale yellow, then mix with the water.
3. Blend the egg and water mixture with the flour, mixing until smooth. Set aside for one hour.
4. Whip the cream and gently stir into the batter.
5. Beat the egg whites until stiff and fold into the batter with the melted butter.
6. Pour two tablespoons of the batter onto a hot, lightly oiled frypan or griddle. Cook until bubbles appear and begin to break. Turn on the other side and cook until golden.

Makes 20-24.

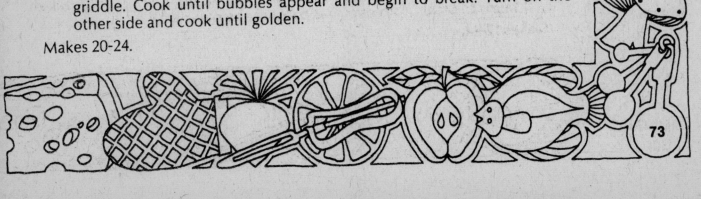

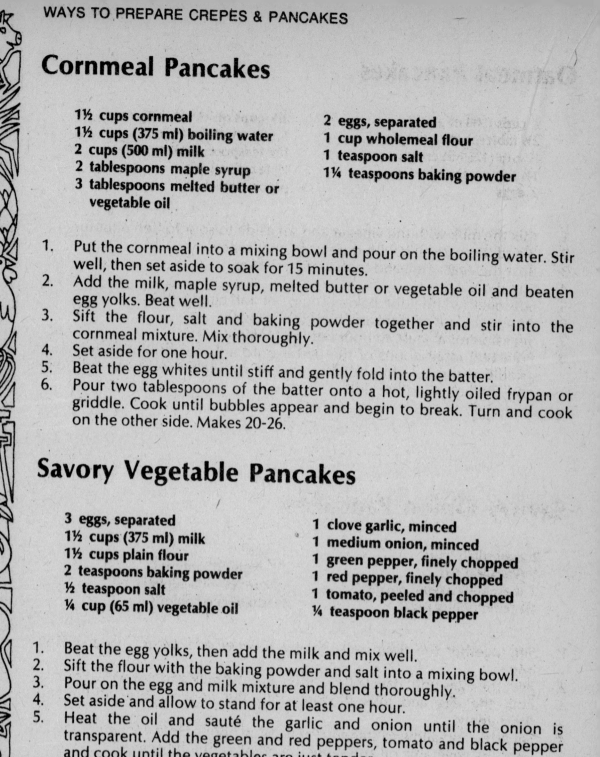

# Cornmeal Pancakes

1½ cups cornmeal
1½ cups (375 ml) boiling water
2 cups (500 ml) milk
2 tablespoons maple syrup
3 tablespoons melted butter or
   vegetable oil

2 eggs, separated
1 cup wholemeal flour
1 teaspoon salt
1¼ teaspoons baking powder

1. Put the cornmeal into a mixing bowl and pour on the boiling water. Stir well, then set aside to soak for 15 minutes.
2. Add the milk, maple syrup, melted butter or vegetable oil and beaten egg yolks. Beat well.
3. Sift the flour, salt and baking powder together and stir into the cornmeal mixture. Mix thoroughly.
4. Set aside for one hour.
5. Beat the egg whites until stiff and gently fold into the batter.
6. Pour two tablespoons of the batter onto a hot, lightly oiled frypan or griddle. Cook until bubbles appear and begin to break. Turn and cook on the other side. Makes 20-26.

# Savory Vegetable Pancakes

3 eggs, separated
1½ cups (375 ml) milk
1½ cups plain flour
2 teaspoons baking powder
½ teaspoon salt
¼ cup (65 ml) vegetable oil

1 clove garlic, minced
1 medium onion, minced
1 green pepper, finely chopped
1 red pepper, finely chopped
1 tomato, peeled and chopped
¼ teaspoon black pepper

1. Beat the egg yolks, then add the milk and mix well.
2. Sift the flour with the baking powder and salt into a mixing bowl.
3. Pour on the egg and milk mixture and blend thoroughly.
4. Set aside and allow to stand for at least one hour.
5. Heat the oil and sauté the garlic and onion until the onion is transparent. Add the green and red peppers, tomato and black pepper and cook until the vegetables are just tender.
6. Stir the vegetables into the batter.
7. Beat the egg whites until stiff and gently fold into the batter.
8. Pour about three tablespoons of the batter onto a hot, lightly oiled frypan or griddle and cook until bubbles appear and begin to break. Turn over and cook on the other side. Makes 12-14.

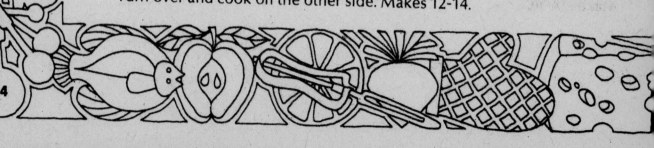

# Oatmeal Pancakes

2 cups (500 ml) milk
2½ tablespoons vinegar
½ cup (125 ml) cream
1¼ tablespoons honey
2 eggs

2½ cups quick-cooking oats
1 cup wholemeal flour
1¼ teaspoons baking soda
½ teaspoon salt
pinch cinnamon

1. Mix the milk with the vinegar and set aside to sour for ten minutes.
2. Blend the sour milk with the cream and honey.
3. Beat the eggs, then add to the milk mixture.
4. Stir in the oats.
5. Sift together the flour, baking soda, salt and cinnamon.
6. Add to the oat mixture and blend thoroughly.
7. Set aside for at least an hour before cooking.
8. Pour two tablespoons of the batter onto a hot, lightly oiled frypan or griddle and cook until bubbles appear and begin to break. Turn over and cook on the other side.

Makes 18-20.

# Savory Onion Pancakes

2 cups plain flour
1 teaspoon salt
2 teaspoons baking powder
1¼ tablespoons sugar

2 eggs
1½ cups (375 ml) milk
¼ cup (65 ml) vegetable oil
1 cup minced onions

1. Sift together the flour, salt, baking powder and sugar into a mixing bowl.
2. Beat the eggs until pale yellow, then add the milk and mix well.
3. Pour the egg and milk mixture onto the flour mixture and blend thoroughly.
4. Set aside and allow to stand for at least an hour before cooking.
5. Heat the vegetable oil and sauté the onions until transparent.
6. Stir into the batter.
7. Pour three tablespoons of the batter onto a hot, lightly oiled frypan or griddle. Cook until bubbles appear and begin to break. Turn over and cook on the other side.

Makes 14-16.

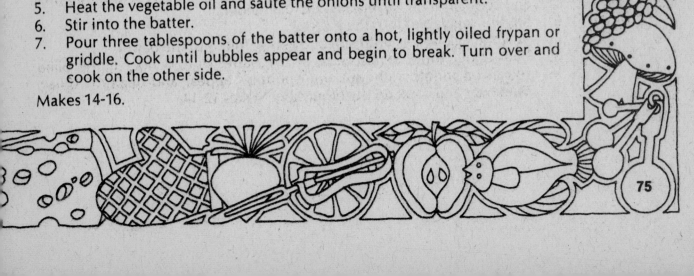

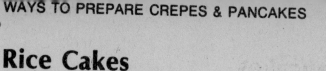

# Rice Cakes

1½ cups plain flour
1½ teaspoons baking powder
½ teaspoon salt
2½ tablespoons sugar
pinch nutmeg

¼ teaspoon cinnamon
½ cup cooked rice, cooled
1 egg
1 cup (250 ml) milk
2½ tablespoons melted butter

1. Sift together the flour, baking powder, salt, sugar, nutmeg and cinnamon.
2. Stir in the rice.
3. Beat the egg until pale yellow, then mix with the milk.
4. Pour the egg and milk mixture into the rice mixture and beat well.
5. Add the melted butter and blend thoroughly.
6. Set aside for at least an hour before cooking.
7. Pour two tablespoons of the batter onto a hot, lightly oiled frypan or griddle. Cook until bubbles appear and begin to break. Turn and cook on the other side.

Makes 12-16.

# Cheesey Pancakes

3 eggs
¾ cup (185 ml) water
1 cup cake flour
½ teaspoon salt

1 cup grated Cheddar cheese
1¼ tablespoons melted butter or vegetable oil
chopped parsley

1. Beat the eggs until pale yellow. Pour in the water and continue beating.
2. Sift the flour and salt into a mixing bowl.
3. Add the egg and water mixture and beat well.
4. Stir in the grated cheese and melted butter or vegetable oil.
5. Allow to stand for at least an hour before cooking.
6. Stir a few times and pour three tablespoons of the batter onto a hot, lightly oiled frypan or griddle. Cook until bubbles appear and begin to break. Turn and cook on the other side. Serve sprinkled with chopped parsley.

Makes 12-15.

# Cottage Cheese Pancakes

3 eggs
¾ cup (185 ml) water
½ cup cake flour
½ teaspoon salt

⅓ cup sugar
1½ cups (375 g) cottage cheese
2½ tablespoons vegetable oil
melted butter

1. Beat the eggs until pale yellow.
2. Add the water and beat well.
3. Sift together the flour, salt and sugar into a mixing bowl.
4. Pour on the egg and water mixture and mix thoroughly.
5. Stir in the cottage cheese and vegetable oil and set aside for at least one hour.
6. Pour two or three tablespoons of the batter onto a hot, lightly oiled frypan or griddle and cook until bubbles appear and begin to break. Turn and cook on the other side. Serve with melted butter.

Makes 14-18.

# Choco-Cakes

2 cups plain flour
2 tablespoons cocoa
2¼ teaspoons baking powder
¾ teaspoon salt

2 eggs, separated
2 tablespoons sugar
1¼ cups (300 ml) milk
confectioner's sugar

1. Sift together the flour, cocoa, baking powder and salt into a mixing bowl.
2. Beat the egg yolks with the sugar until thick and creamy.
3. Add the milk to the egg yolk mixture and beat well.
4. Pour into the flour mixture and blend thoroughly.
5. Set aside and allow to stand for at least one hour.
6. Beat the egg whites until stiff and gently fold into the batter.
7. Pour three tablespoons of the batter onto a hot, lightly oiled frypan or griddle. Cook until bubbles appear and begin to break. Turn and cook on the other side.
8. Serve sprinkled with confectioner's sugar.

Makes 12-14.

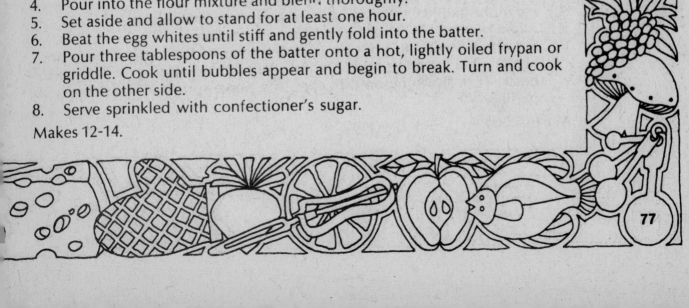

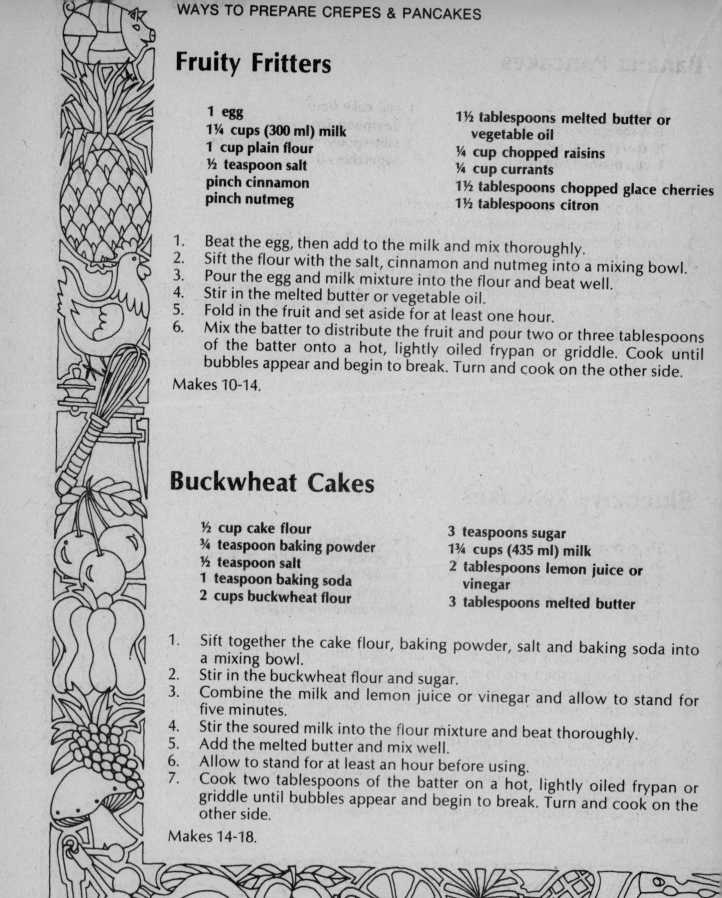

# Fruity Fritters

1 egg
1¼ cups (300 ml) milk
1 cup plain flour
½ teaspoon salt
pinch cinnamon
pinch nutmeg

1½ tablespoons melted butter or
  vegetable oil
¼ cup chopped raisins
¼ cup currants
1½ tablespoons chopped glace cherries
1½ tablespoons citron

1. Beat the egg, then add to the milk and mix thoroughly.
2. Sift the flour with the salt, cinnamon and nutmeg into a mixing bowl.
3. Pour the egg and milk mixture into the flour and beat well.
4. Stir in the melted butter or vegetable oil.
5. Fold in the fruit and set aside for at least one hour.
6. Mix the batter to distribute the fruit and pour two or three tablespoons of the batter onto a hot, lightly oiled frypan or griddle. Cook until bubbles appear and begin to break. Turn and cook on the other side.

Makes 10-14.

# Buckwheat Cakes

½ cup cake flour
¾ teaspoon baking powder
½ teaspoon salt
1 teaspoon baking soda
2 cups buckwheat flour

3 teaspoons sugar
1¾ cups (435 ml) milk
2 tablespoons lemon juice or
  vinegar
3 tablespoons melted butter

1. Sift together the cake flour, baking powder, salt and baking soda into a mixing bowl.
2. Stir in the buckwheat flour and sugar.
3. Combine the milk and lemon juice or vinegar and allow to stand for five minutes.
4. Stir the soured milk into the flour mixture and beat thoroughly.
5. Add the melted butter and mix well.
6. Allow to stand for at least an hour before using.
7. Cook two tablespoons of the batter on a hot, lightly oiled frypan or griddle until bubbles appear and begin to break. Turn and cook on the other side.

Makes 14-18.

# Banana Pancakes

3 eggs
1½ tablespoons honey
½ cup (125 ml) milk
1 cup mashed bananas

1 cup cake flour
½ teaspoon salt
3 tablespoons melted butter or
vegetable oil

1. Beat together the eggs, honey and milk.
2. Add the mashed bananas and mix well.
3. Sift the flour and salt into the banana mixture. Blend thoroughly.
4. Stir in the melted butter or vegetable oil.
5. Set aside and allow to stand for at least an hour.
6. Pour two tablespoons of the batter onto a hot, lightly oiled frypan or griddle. Cook until bubbles appear and begin to break. Turn over and cook on the other side.

Makes 20.

# Blueberry Pancakes

1¼ cups plain flour
½ teaspoon salt
1 tablespoon baking powder
1¼ tablespoons sugar
1 egg

1 cup (250 ml) milk
2½ tablespoons melted butter or
vegetable oil
½ cup drained blueberries
butter and brown sugar

1. Sift the flour, salt, baking powder and sugar into a mixing bowl.
2. Beat the egg, then add to the milk and mix well.
3. Mix the egg and milk mixture with the flour mixture.
4. Add the melted butter or vegetable oil and blueberries. Blend thoroughly.
5. Set aside and allow to stand for at least an hour.
6. Pour two tablespoons of the batter onto a hot lightly oiled frypan or griddle. Cook until bubbles appear and begin to break. Turn over and cook on the other side.
7. Spread with butter, sprinkle with brown sugar and serve immediately.

Makes 12-15.

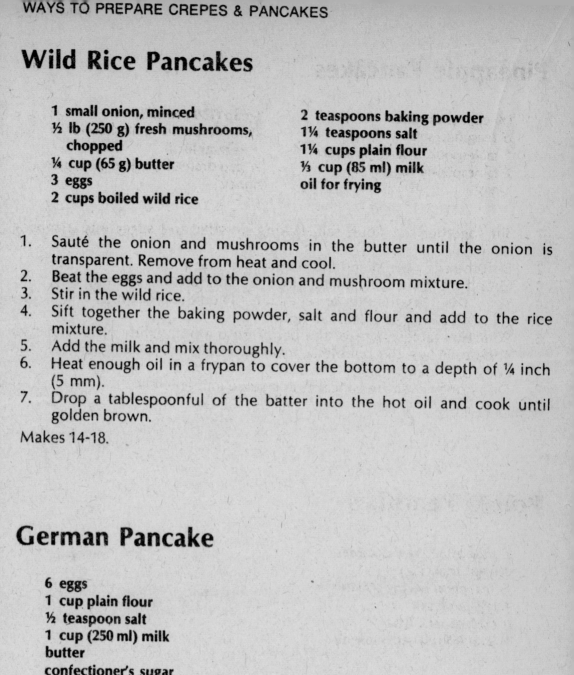

# Wild Rice Pancakes

1 small onion, minced
½ lb (250 g) fresh mushrooms, chopped
¼ cup (65 g) butter
3 eggs
2 cups boiled wild rice

2 teaspoons baking powder
1¼ teaspoons salt
1¼ cups plain flour
⅓ cup (85 ml) milk
oil for frying

1. Sauté the onion and mushrooms in the butter until the onion is transparent. Remove from heat and cool.
2. Beat the eggs and add to the onion and mushroom mixture.
3. Stir in the wild rice.
4. Sift together the baking powder, salt and flour and add to the rice mixture.
5. Add the milk and mix thoroughly.
6. Heat enough oil in a frypan to cover the bottom to a depth of ¼ inch (5 mm).
7. Drop a tablespoonful of the batter into the hot oil and cook until golden brown.

Makes 14-18.

# German Pancake

6 eggs
1 cup plain flour
½ teaspoon salt
1 cup (250 ml) milk
butter
confectioner's sugar
lemon juice

1. Beat the eggs until light and pale yellow.
2. Sift the flour with the salt and add to the eggs alternately with the milk. Beat constantly.
3. Generously butter the bottom and sides of a 10-inch (25-cm) pan.
4. Pour in the batter and bake in a 400°F (200°C) oven for about 20 minutes.
5. Serve sprinkled with confectioner's sugar and lemon juice.

# Pineapple Pancakes

1¼ cups plain flour
½ teaspoon salt
1 tablespoon baking powder
2 tablespoons sugar
1 egg

1 cup (250 ml) milk
2½ tablespoons melted butter or
   vegetable oil
½ cup drained crushed pineapple
honey

1. Sift together the flour, salt, baking powder and sugar into a mixing bowl.
2. Beat the egg, then blend thoroughly with the milk.
3. Pour the egg and milk mixture into the flour mixture and mix well.
4. Stir in the melted butter or vegetable oil and the pineapple.
5. Allow to stand for at least an hour.
6. Pour two tablespoons of the batter onto a hot, lightly oiled frypan or griddle. When the bubbles appear and begin to break, turn over and cook on the other side.
7. Drip honey over the pancakes and serve immediately.

Makes 12-14.

# Potato Pancakes

2 cups grated raw potatoes
2 eggs, separated
½ teaspoon baking powder
1 teaspoon salt
2 tablespoons flour
¼ cup (65 ml) vegetable oil

1. Peel the potatoes and soak in cold water for at least two hours.
2. Grate the potatoes and drain well. This draining removes the starch.
3. Beat the egg yolks until pale yellow and add to the grated potatoes.
4. Sift together the baking powder, salt and flour.
5. Add to the potato mixture and blend thoroughly.
6. Beat the egg whites until stiff and fold into the potato mixture.
7. Heat the vegetable oil in a frypan until very hot. Drop in the batter by the spoonful and cook until golden brown.
8. Drain on absorbent paper and serve immediately.

Makes about 12.

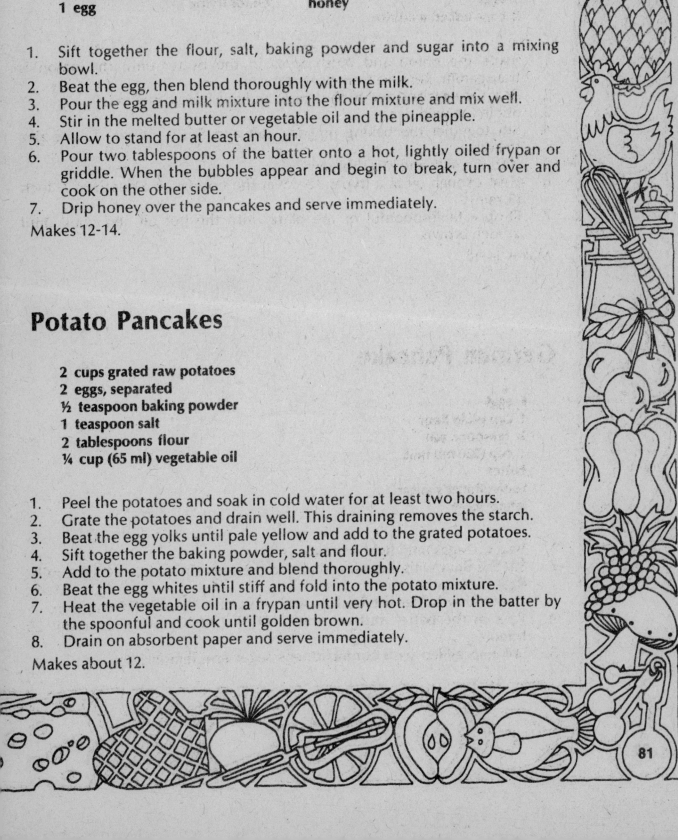

# Scottish Pancakes

1 cup cake flour
2 tablespoons sugar
1 egg
⅔ cup (165 ml) buttermilk

1. Sift together the flour and sugar into a mixing bowl.
2. Beat the egg until pale yellow, then mix with the buttermilk.
3. Pour the egg and buttermilk mixture onto the flour and blend thoroughly.
4. Set aside for at least an hour before cooking.
5. Pour two tablespoons of the batter onto a hot, lightly oiled frypan or griddle and cook until bubbles appear and begin to break. Turn and cook on the other side.

Makes 14-18.

# Waffles

## Basic Waffle Recipe

2 cups plain flour
2¼ teaspoons baking powder
½ teaspoon salt
3 eggs, separated

1⅔ cups (415 ml) milk
¼ cup (65 ml) melted butter or
vegetable oil

1. Sift together the flour, baking powder and salt into a mixing bowl.
2. Beat the egg yolks until pale yellow, then add to the milk and beat well.
3. Pour the egg yolk and milk mixture onto the flour and blend thoroughly.
4. Stir in the melted butter or vegetable oil.
5. Set aside for about an hour.
6. Beat the egg whites until stiff and fold into the batter.
7. Fill a hot lightly oiled waffle iron two-thirds full with the batter. Cook until the steam stops escaping from the sides.

Makes 4-8.

# Wonderful Waffles

2 cups plain flour
2 teaspoons baking powder
½ teaspoon salt
1 teaspoon baking soda

2 teaspoons sugar
3 eggs, separated
1 cup (250 ml) sour cream
1 cup (250 ml) milk

1. Sift together the flour, baking powder, salt, baking soda and sugar into a mixing bowl.
2. Beat the egg yolks until pale yellow.
3. Mix the sour cream with the milk, then beat in the egg yolks.
4. Add to the sifted dry ingredients. Set aside for at least one hour.
5. Beat the egg whites until stiff and fold into the batter.
6. Fill a hot, lightly oiled waffle iron two-thirds full with the batter and cook until no more steam is emerging from the sides.

Makes 4-8.

# Egg Waffles

⅔ cup plain flour
¼ cup (65 ml) water
4 eggs, separated
½ teaspoon salt

pinch of black pepper
2½ tablespoons melted butter or
    bacon fat

1. Blend together the flour and water.
2. Beat the egg yolks until pale yellow, then add to the flour and water mixture.
3. Stir in the salt, pepper and melted butter or bacon fat.
4. Set aside and allow to stand for at least an hour.
5. Beat the egg whites until stiff and gently fold into the batter.
6. Fill a hot lightly oiled waffle iron two-thirds full with the batter and cook for about 3-4 minutes or until the steam stops escaping.

Makes 2-4.

# Sweet Milk Waffles

| | |
|---|---|
| 2 cups plain flour | 3 eggs, separated |
| 2 tablespoons sugar | 2 cups (500 ml) milk |
| 1 tablespoons baking powder | 2½ tablespoons sugar |
| ½ teaspoon salt | ½ cup (125 ml) melted butter |

1. Sift together the flour, sugar, baking powder and salt into a mixing bowl.
2. Beat the egg yolks until pale yellow.
3. Gently heat the milk and the sugar until the sugar dissolves. Cool.
4. Pour the egg yolks, cooled milk and the melted butter into the flour mixture. Stir until smooth.
5. Set aside and allow to stand for at least an hour.
6. Beat the egg whites until stiff. Carefully fold into the batter.
7. Fill a hot lightly oiled waffle iron two-thirds full with the batter and cook until the steam stops escaping.

Makes 4-8.

# Ham Waffles

| | |
|---|---|
| 2 cups plain flour | 1¾ cups (435 ml) milk |
| 1 tablespoon baking powder | ⅓ cup (85 ml) melted butter, |
| 1 teaspoon salt | bacon fat or vegetable oil |
| 2 eggs, separated | ¾ cup minced ham |

1. Sift together the flour, baking powder and salt into a mixing bowl.
2. Beat the egg yolks until pale yellow, then combine with the milk.
3. Stir the egg and milk mixture into the flour.
4. Add the melted butter, bacon fat or vegetable and the minced ham. Blend thoroughly.
5. Set aside and allow to stand for at least one hour.
6. Beat the egg whites until stiff and gently fold into the batter.
7. Pour on enough batter to fill a hot lightly oiled waffle iron two-thirds full with the batter. Cook until the steam stops escaping.

Makes 4-8.

# Potato Waffles

3 eggs
1 cup plain flour
2 teaspoons baking powder
½ teaspoon salt

1 cup (250 ml) milk
1½ tablespoons melted butter or
   vegetable oil
2 cups grated raw potatoes

1. Beat the eggs until pale yellow.
2. Sift the flour, baking powder and salt and add to the eggs.
3. Stir in the milk, melted butter or vegetable oil and potatoes. Blend thoroughly.
4. Fill a hot lightly oiled waffle iron two-thirds full with the batter and cook until the steam stops escaping.

Makes 4-8

# Golden Coconut Waffles

2 cups plain flour
2¼ teaspoons baking powder
½ teaspoon salt
3 eggs, separated
2½ cups (375 ml) milk

2½ tablespoons maple syrup
¼ cup (65 ml) melted butter or
   vegetable oil
⅔ cup desiccated coconut

1. Sift the flour with the baking powder and salt into a mixing bowl.
2. Beat the egg yolks until pale yellow, then mix with the milk and maple syrup.
3. Pour the egg yolk and milk mixture onto the flour and blend thoroughly.
4. Stir in the melted butter or vegetable oil.
5. Allow to stand for at least an hour.
6. Beat the egg whites until stiff and fold into the batter with the desiccated coconut.
7. Fill a hot, lightly oiled waffle iron two-thirds full with the batter and cook until the steam no longer escapes from the sides.

Makes 4-8

# Banana Waffles

2 cups plain flour
2¼ teaspoons baking powder
½ teaspoon salt
¼ teaspoon nutmeg
3 eggs, separated

1⅓ cups (415 ml) milk
¼ cup (65 ml) melted butter or
   vegetable oil
⅔ cup mashed bananas

1.  Sift together the flour, baking powder, salt and nutmeg into a mixing bowl.
2.  Beat the egg yolks until pale yellow, then add the milk and beat well.
3.  Pour the egg yolk and milk mixture onto the flour and blend thoroughly.
4.  Stir in the melted butter or vegetable oil.
5.  Set aside for at least an hour.
6.  Mix the mashed bananas with the batter.
7.  Beat the egg whites until stiff and fold into the banana batter.
8.  Fill a hot, lightly oiled waffle iron two-thirds full with the batter and cook until the steam stops escaping from the sides.

Makes 4-8.

# Lemon Waffles

2 cups plain flour
2¼ teaspoons baking powder
½ teaspoon salt
3 eggs, separated
1½ cups (375 ml) milk

2½ tablespoons lemon juice
1¼ tablespoons grated lemon rind
¼ cup (65 ml) melted butter or
   vegetable oil

1.  Sift together the flour, baking powder and salt into a mixing bowl.
2.  Beat the egg yolks until pale yellow and mix with the milk.
3.  Pour the egg yolk and milk mixture onto the flour and mix well.
4.  Add the lemon juice and grated lemon rind and blend thoroughly.
5.  Stir in the melted butter or vegetable oil.
6.  Set aside for at least an hour.
7.  Beat the egg whites until stiff and fold into the batter.
8.  Fill a hot, lightly oiled waffle iron two-thirds full with the batter. Cook until the steam ceases to escape from the sides of the waffle iron.

Makes 4-8.

# Buttermilk Waffles

2 cups plain flour
2¼ teaspoons baking powder
½ teaspoon salt
3 eggs, separated

1½ cups (375 ml) buttermilk
2½ tablespoons honey
¼ cup (65 ml) melted butter or
   vegetable oil

1. Sift the flour with the baking powder and salt into a mixing bowl.
2. Beat the egg yolks until pale yellow, then add to the buttermilk and beat well.
3. Pour the egg yolk and milk mixture onto the flour and blend thoroughly.
4. Stir in the honey and melted butter or vegetable oil.
5. Set aside for at least an hour.
6. Beat the egg whites until stiff and fold into the batter.
7. Fill a hot, lightly oiled waffle iron two-thirds full with the batter. Cook until the steam stops escaping from the sides.

Makes 4-8.

# Wholemeal Waffles

2 eggs, separated
1½ cups (375 ml) milk
1½ cups wholemeal flour
½ teaspoon salt

2 teaspoons baking powder
2½ tablespoons honey
2½ tablespoons melted butter or
   vegetable oil

1. Beat the egg yolks until pale yellow.
2. Add the milk to the egg yolks and beat well.
3. Sift the flour with the salt and baking powder into a mixing bowl.
4. Add the egg yolk and milk mixture and blend thoroughly.
5. Stir in the honey and melted butter or vegetable oil.
6. Allow to stand for at least an hour.
7. Beat the egg whites until stiff and fold into the batter.
8. Pour enough batter onto a hot lightly oiled waffle iron two-thirds full with the batter and cook until the steam stops escaping from the sides.

Makes 4-8.

# Choc-Waffles

2½ cups plain flour
1 tablespoon baking powder
½ teaspoon salt
2½ tablespoons cocoa
5 tablespoons sugar

2 eggs, separated
1½ cups (375 ml) milk
¼ teaspoon vanilla essence
4 tablespoons melted butter or
vegetable oil

1. Sift together the flour, baking powder, salt, cocoa and sugar into a mixing bowl.
2. Beat the egg yolks until pale yellow.
3. Pour the milk onto the egg yolks and beat thoroughly.
4. Mix the egg yolk and milk mixture with the flour mixture.
5. Stir in the vanilla essence and the melted butter or vegetable oil.
6. Set aside for at least an hour.
7. Beat the egg whites until stiff and fold into the batter.
8. Fill a hot, oiled waffle iron two-thirds full with the batter and cook until the steam stops escaping from the sides.

Makes 4-8.

# Bacon Waffles

2 cups plain flour
2¼ teaspoons baking powder
½ teaspoon salt
3 eggs, separated

1⅔ cups (415 ml) milk
¼ cup (65 ml) melted butter or
vegetable oil
⅔ cup cooked bacon bits

1. Sift together the flour, baking powder and salt into a mixing bowl.
2. Beat the egg yolks until pale yellow, then add to the milk and beat well.
3. Pour the egg yolk and milk mixture onto the flour and blend thoroughly.
4. Stir in the melted butter or vegetable.
5. Set aside for about an hour.
6. Beat the egg whites until stiff and fold into the batter with the bacon pieces.
7. Fill a hot, oiled waffle iron two-thirds full and cook until the steam stops escaping from the sides.

Makes 4-8.

# Cheesey Waffles

2 cups plain flour
2¼ teaspoons baking powder
½ teaspoon salt
3 eggs, separated

1⅓ cups (415 ml) milk
¼ cup (65 ml) melted butter or
  vegetable oil
⅔ cup grated Cheddar cheese

1. Sift the flour with the baking powder and salt into a mixing bowl.
2. Beat the egg yolks until pale yellow, then add to the milk and beat well.
3. Pour the egg yolk and milk mixture onto the flour and blend thoroughly.
4. Stir in the melted butter or vegetable oil.
5. Set aside and allow to stand for about an hour.
6. Beat the egg whites until stiff and fold into the batter with the grated cheese.
7. Fill a hot, lightly oiled waffle iron two-thirds full with the batter and cook until the steam stops escaping from the sides.

Makes 4-8.

# Nutty Waffles

2 cups plain flour
2¼ teaspoons baking powder
½ teaspoon salt
½ teaspoon ground cinnamon
3 eggs, separated

1⅓ cups (415 ml) milk
¼ cup (65 ml) melted butter or
  vegetable oil
⅔ cup chopped nuts

1. Sift together the flour, baking powder, salt and cinnamon.
2. Beat the egg yolks until pale yellow, then add to the milk and beat well.
3. Pour the egg yolk and milk mixture onto the flour and blend thoroughly.
4. Stir in the melted butter or vegetable oil.
5. Allow to stand for at least an hour.
6. Beat the egg whites until stiff and fold into the batter with the chopped nuts.
7. Fill a hot, lightly oiled waffle iron until two-thirds full with the batter. Cook until the steam stops escaping from the sides.

Makes 4-8.

# Strawberry Waffles

2 cups plain flour
2¼ teaspoons baking powder
½ teaspoon salt
3 eggs, separated

1⅔ cups (415 ml) milk
¼ cup (65 ml) melted butter or
  vegetable oil
⅔ cup chopped fresh strawberries

1. Sift together the flour, baking powder and salt into a mixing bowl.
2. Beat the egg yolks until pale yellow, then mix thoroughly with the milk.
3. Pour the egg yolk and milk mixture onto the flour and blend thoroughly.
4. Stir in the melted butter or vegetable oil.
5. Set aside for at least an hour.
6. Beat the egg whites until stiff and fold into the batter with the chopped strawberries.
7. Fill a hot, lightly oiled waffle iron until two-thirds full with the batter. Cook until the steam stops escaping from the sides.

Makes 4-8.

# Corn Waffles

1¾ cups plain flour
½ teaspoon salt
1 tablespoon baking powder
1¼ tablespoons sugar
2 eggs, separated

1 cup (250 ml) milk
2½ tablespoons melted butter or
  vegetable oil
2 cups canned creamed corn

1. Sift the dry ingredients into a mixing bowl.
2. Beat the egg yolks with the milk and add to the flour.
3. Stir in the melted butter or vegetable oil and creamed corn. Mix thoroughly.
4. Set aside and allow to stand for at least one hour.
5. Beat the egg whites until stiff and fold into the batter.
6. Fill a hot, lightly oiled waffle iron two-thirds full with the batter and cook until the steam no longer escapes from the sides.

Makes 4-8.

# Corn Flake Waffles

1¼ cups plain flour
½ teaspoon salt
1 tablespoon baking powder
¾ cup cornflake crumbs

1¼ cups (300 ml) milk
2 eggs, separated
2½ tablespoons melted butter or
vegetable oil

1. Sift together the flour, salt and baking powder into a mixing bowl.
2. Add the cornflake crumbs and blend thoroughly.
3. Beat the egg yolks with the milk and stir into the flour and corn flake crumb mixture.
4. Add the melted butter or vegetable oil and beat well.
5. Set aside and allow to stand for at least one hour.
6. Beat the egg whites until stiff and fold into the batter.
7. Fill a hot lightly oiled waffle iron until it is two-thirds full with the batter. Cook until steam no longer escapes from the sides.

Makes 4-8.

# Super Duper Waffles

2½ cups plain flour
¾ teaspoon salt
1¼ tablespoons baking powder
2½ tablespoons sugar

2 eggs, beaten
2 cups (500 ml) milk
⅔ cup (165 ml) melted butter or
vegetable oil

1. Sift together the dry ingredients into a mixing bowl.
2. Combine the eggs, milk and melted butter or vegetable oil.
3. Pour the milk mixture into the mixing bowl with the flour and beat until smooth. Set aside for one hour.
4. Fill a hot lightly oiled waffle iron two-thirds full with the batter and cook until no more steam is escaping.
5. Serve with Honey Sauce.

Makes 8-14.

Honey Sauce:
Gently heat together 1 cup honey, ¼ cup (65 g) butter, ½ teaspoon cinnamon and ⅛ teaspoon of nutmeg in the top of a double boiler over simmering water. Pour over waffles and serve immediately.

# Sour Cream Waffles

1 cup plain flour
¼ teaspoon salt
½ teaspoon baking soda
2 teaspoons sugar

1 large egg, separated
1 cup (250 g) sour cream
1¼ tablespoons melted butter or
   vegetable oil

1. Sift together the flour, salt, baking soda and sugar into a mixing bowl.
2. Combine the egg yolk with the sour cream and stir into the flour mixture.
3. Beat in the melted butter or vegetable oil.
4. Set aside and allow to stand for at least an hour.
5. Beat the egg white until stiff and fold into the batter.
6. Fill a hot lightly oiled waffle iron two-thirds full with the batter and cook until steam no longer appears.

Makes 4-6.

# Dessert Waffles

1 cup cake flour
½ teaspoon salt
1 tablespoon baking powder
2½ tablespoons sugar
2 eggs
1 cup (250 ml) cream
2 egg whites

1. Sift together the flour, salt, baking powder and sugar into a mixing bowl.
2. Beat the two eggs until pale yellow.
3. Add the cream and mix thoroughly.
4. Beat the egg mixture into the flour mixture until smooth.
5. Set aside for at least one hour.
6. Beat the egg whites until stiff and fold into the batter.
7. Fill a hot lightly oiled waffle iron until two-thirds full with the batter. Cook until no more steam escapes.

Makes 4-8.

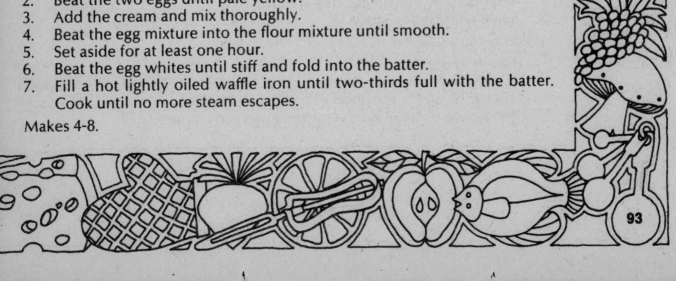

# Crisp Waffles

| | |
|---|---|
| 2 cups cake flour | 1 cup (250 ml) milk |
| 1¼ tablespoons baking powder | ½ cup (125 ml) cream |
| ½ teaspoon salt | 2 eggs, separated |
| 1 tablespoon sugar | ⅔ cup (165 ml) melted butter |

1. Sift together the flour, baking powder, salt and sugar into a mixing bowl. Sift again.
2. Combine the milk and cream and stir into the flour mixture.
3. Beat the egg yolks until pale yellow.
4. Stir the egg yolks into the batter with the melted butter.
5. Set aside and allow to stand for one hour.
6. Beat the egg whites until stiff and gently fold into the batter.
7. Fill a hot lightly oiled waffle iron two-thirds full with the batter and cook until steam no longer appears.

Makes 4-8.

# Extra Rich Waffles

| | |
|---|---|
| 2 cups plain flour | 3 eggs, separated |
| 2½ tablespoons sugar | 1½ cups (375 ml) milk |
| 1 tablespoon baking powder | ½ cup (125 ml) melted butter or |
| 1 teaspoon salt | bacon fat |

1. Sift together the flour, sugar, baking powder and salt into a mixing bowl.
2. Beat the egg yolks until pale yellow, then combine with the milk.
3. Pour the egg and milk mixture into the flour and stir until smooth.
4. Add the melted butter or bacon fat and blend thoroughly.
5. Set aside and allow to stand for at least an hour.
6. Beat the egg whites until stiff and fold into the batter.
7. Fill a hot lightly oiled waffle iron two-thirds full with the batter and cook until steam stops escaping from the sides.

Makes 4-8.

# Index

# WAYS TO PREPARE CREPES & PANCAKES

NA-B8O96-2/64